15 Life-Related
DRAMAS

for Use in Worship
and Other Congregational
Settings

Theodore W. Schroeder

CPH®
SAINT LOUIS

1 2 3 4 5 6 7 8 9 10   05 04 03 02 01 00 99 98 97 96

Contents

Introduction

Drama in Worship

All of the dramas in this book have been used in worship. Although they can stand alone and can be used in other settings, they are effective as part of a worship experience. Drama in itself cannot create effective worship, but it can make a significant contribution to creating a meaningful worship experience.

■ Drama is one way of communicating. It has strengths that some other ways of "getting the word out" do not have, for instance:

1. **Drama engages people** because it tells a story. It pulls people in as it gives a glimpse into characters' lives. As such, it allows the viewer to connect what is happening in the drama with his or her own life.

2. **Drama evokes emotion.** Unlike some other portions of the worship experience that tend to be intellectual, cognitive, and linear in nature—drama is experiential; it involves the affect. Drama invites the viewer into an experience—an experience that has meaning.

3. **Drama conveys several levels of meaning.** While drama tells a story, it also acts as a metaphor. It carries meaning inside of meaning. It invites the viewer to find his or her own meaning.

4. **Drama enhances the worship experience.** Drama "makes the point" of the service in another way—a way that has special meaning to those who learn experientially, globally, through feelings and emotions. Not every person who populates the pew is an aural, linear learner. Some, especially children, need other

kinds of communication to get and keep meaning.

■ Drama in worship, however, must have certain characteristics, such as the following, to be effective:

1. **Drama must "fit" the theme of worship.** Like music, drama can be that evocative experience in the worship setting that opens the heart of the worshiper and creates a "place" (cognitively and emotionally) for the spoken Word to touch.

2. **Drama must be drama.** Putting a "sermon" in the mouth of several characters will not do. Dialog sermons have a place, but they are not drama. Using a skit will not do. A skit is essentially dialog between two voices around some issue. Skits do have their place—entertainment, if nothing else. But since they are essentially word plays, they are not drama and generally not effective in worship. Drama in worship should have most of the following aspects of longer, dramatic productions:

- There should be integrity to the drama—it should have a point and make it. All of the dialog should move toward the single point.

- It should have authentic characters—and the characters should "develop" during the drama—even in a short drama of only a few minutes.

- The drama should turn on a real issue or conflict—something that touches the life of the viewer.

- The drama should give a sense of story. There should be a beginning, a growing tension, a climax or resolution, and an end. The viewer should have a sense that what he or she has seen is complete—even in a short drama.

- The drama should convey real emotion. Whether the drama evokes joy, sadness, wonder, grief, or laughter—the emotion needs to be integral to the drama and flow from the exchange between the characters. Drama does not set out to be sad or happy or funny. Those emotions, since they are a part of human experience, are a part of good drama.

3. **Drama must focus on character and relationship.** Done in a worship setting, drama cannot be "setting" dependent. Sets and scenes are suggested with only minimal props, and the drama can only be minimally "action" dependent. Chases, races, and broad actions will not fit the chancel. The drama focuses on character and conflict.

4. **Drama must be effective.** Not every exchange of words between two characters in front of an audience is drama. Drama requires that the exchange be "true"—that is, "true to life," not necessarily factual. Drama speaks real and effectively enough to invite the viewer into the dramatic action.

5. **Drama must be brief.** Drama in worship is only part of the experience. It cannot dominate the worship hour. It finds its place in making the worship ready for the spoken Word or by reinforcing the spoken Word. It does not attempt to be the "center of attention."

■ You will find the dramas in this book effective in worship for these reasons:

- They are brief. They can be done in 4–10 minutes.

- They are character centered. They focus on conflict and change that real people experience.

- They are "pointed." They drive toward a single concept or idea.

- They are real. They deal with real conflicts in the lives of real people.

- They are not set or costume dependent. Only enough props are needed to suggest a setting. A chair suggests a living room. A table with clothing on it suggests a store.

- They require only a few (up to four) actors. Most of the parts, with only minor adjustments in the dialog, can be done by males or females.

- They require little rehearsal time.

Guidelines for Using Drama in Worship

These dramas can be used in a worship setting. The following are general guidelines for using these dramas and others like them:

1. Choose the drama carefully. Don't use a drama just because you have some time to fill. The drama needs to fit the point and purpose of the worship service.

2. Place the drama carefully. Does it help prepare the worshiper for worship? Use it toward the beginning of the service. Does it emphasize the message from the Word? Use it following the sermon.

3. Allow the drama to "work." Don't rush it. Present it carefully. Allow time afterward for reflection.

Production Notes

1. You don't need a stage, elaborate props, or sophisticated lighting. Darkness will help the production. These dramas focus on character. They work best when the audience' attention can be focused on the actors. Doing the dramas in darkness, with a single spot on the actors, works well. Darkness also helps overcome visual distractions. Darkness and quiet enhance meditation and reflection.

2. If your chancel area is just not suitable for

a dramatic production or if you are unable to control lighting—an alternative would be to do the dramas ahead of time and videotape them. Showing the video on a large-screen monitor becomes the means to convey the drama in worship.

3. Props and costumes are suggested with each drama. Most of these can be gathered with minimal effort. Often items can be suggested by a picture of them (for instance, instead of using an actual television, use a picture of one).

4. Keep it simple. Depend on "suspension of disbelief" in the audience. It is not necessary to show every aspect of a street corner to make people believe the actors are on a street corner. The recorded sound of traffic will do it, or a street sign. It is not necessary to show a complete cell when the action takes place in a prison or dungeon. The shadow of bars on the floor or the sound of a jail cell door will suffice. To begin the drama, you do not need a "curtain." The actors can simply walk on, or the lights can come up to mark the beginning. Similarly, darkness can make an ending, or the actors can simply walk off. Since the dramas focus on character, the setting need only be suggested. Audi-ences—used to focusing on character—will quickly "get" the setting and focus on the dramatic action.

5. If possible, ask actors to memorize lines. Most of the lines are brief and easily learned. The dramas can, of course, be read from scripts, but lines said from memory give a more powerful, realistic effect.

Getting the Dramas Done

As you begin the use of drama in worship, consider forming a "drama group" in your congregation. Certainly there will be those (including youth) who will be interested in taking part in the dramas, in directing, and in doing sets and costumes. Encourage these people to form an ongoing group that can take responsibility for the production of dramas. The group will take pride in their efforts, and their interest and commitment will make the dramatic productions more effective.

After a time, you will find that your drama group will move toward writing and producing their own dramas. Help them follow the principles of drama in worship outlined above and let them use their creativity to enhance your worship experience.

Advent/Christmas
Two Dramas

These dramas emphasize the "nowness" and "personalness" of the Christmas/incarnation event.

Within My Heart—a traditional drama—will communicate to both children and adults. Jesus said, "Whatever you do to the least of these … you have done it to me." In this play, "the least" is a bag lady who invades—and yet enriches—the life of a lonely woman.

The Coming, though apparently a simple story, is a more metaphorical drama conveying the invasiveness of the incarnation. It tells of the intrusive birth of a child into an unready home. The birth—seemingly accidental—brings healing, as the seemingly accidental birth of Jesus brought healing to the world. The play includes a telling of the Christmas story in pantomime. Adults might find a discussion of the themes and metaphors in the play helpful as they contemplate the meaning of Christmas for their own lives.

Within My Heart

An Advent/Christmas drama in one scene

Characters

Ned—*night watchman in a department store, in uniform*

Mrs. Yancey—*store employee, middle-aged, dressed carefully for work*

Mandy—*elderly bag lady, wearing dirty, tattered clothing*

Scene

The stage is dimly lit. Downstage is a puddle of light—perhaps from a single spotlight—in which most of the action takes place. A few tables stacked with clothing suggest a department store. Near the center of the stage, quite in the shadows, is a large manger scene. It holds figures like those one might find on a lawn. They are in a kind of crèche with straw strewn around.

Ned, the night watchman, wanders through the counters on his rounds, singing.

Ned (*singing softly*): "Watchman, tell us of the night; what its sounds of beauty are …"

(He comes on Yancey who is standing, gazing at the manger scene.)

Ned: Hey, Mrs. Yancey, what are you doing here? Don't you know it's Christmas Eve?

Yancey: Oh, hi, Ned. I was just finishing up some of the sales records. Big week, you know.

Ned: Listen, I don't know a lot about how this store works, but I do know that they can't be paying you enough to keep you here on Christmas Eve.

Yancey: Oh, it's nothing like that Ned. I just want to get a head start on the end of the year work, you know.

Ned: But you don't have to be here on Christmas Eve. All that stuff will wait. I mean, I've got to work. Somebody's got to watch the place. But you can do books any time.

Yancey: I know. (*Pensively.*) But I really don't have anywhere to go this evening, so I might as well get this done.

Ned: Nowhere to go? Isn't your family getting together?

Yancey: No. I … I don't really have any family—at least not around here.

Ned: But your children …

Yancey (*a little embarrassed*): I was married long ago, Ned, and only for a short time. I don't have any children.

Ned: But there should be someone.

Yancey: Oh, I have friends. *(Quieter.)* Lots of friends. But they're—I don't know—they're kind of tied up this evening. So it's just me and Mathilda—and she's not too much into Christmas.

Ned: Mathilda?

Yancey: My cat. She'll be waiting for me at the apartment.

Ned: Gee, that seems kind of a shame—that you're all alone, I mean.

Yancey: You know, it's kind of funny we're talking about this, Ned. Just as you came up, I was there by the manger scene, remembering.

Ned: Remembering?

Yancey: Yeah, I was thinking back to when I was a kid. Christmases were so wonderful then. We'd go to church on Christmas Eve and come home and open what seemed like a mountain of gifts. And then, later in the evening, we'd all gather around the manger scene, and Daddy would tell us the Christmas story—I guess he'd kind of recite it. And we'd sing carols. Then just before we'd go to bed, we'd sing that old carol—it was Daddy's favorite. I'm not sure if I remember it. *(She sings softly.)* "Ah dearest Jesus, holy child, Make thee a bed, soft, undefiled; Within my heart that it may be, A quiet chamber kept for thee." *(Pause.)* Funny, what you remember, isn't it?

Ned: Yeah, I guess I was doing some remembering too. Christmas for me is nothing like it used to be either. Look at me. Here I am wandering around a dark store.

Yancey: I guess I'm too old to find that kind of a Christmas anymore. I guess I should be content with my work and spending the evening with Mathilda. But just once, just once I'd like to feel that glow again that came when it seemed that the baby was born in my home and in my heart …

(There's a rustling sound behind the manger.)

Ned: Here? What's that?

Yancey: I don't know. But I heard it too. *(She reaches for his arm.)* I'm sure glad you're here, Ned.

(Ned pulls away and starts to poke around the stable in the dark. Over by the manger he stumbles over something.)

Ned: Here—what's this? Here—you there—come out of there! I've got you. No tricks now.

Mandy (*standing slowly*): Now don't get excited! I'm not going to do anything. Just take it easy.

Yancey: Who is it, Ned?

Ned: It's an old woman—right here in the manger scene. She's … she's …

Mandy: Kind of ratty looking—isn't that what you were going to say? I'm kind of down and dirty and all messed up.

(*Ned leads the old woman into the light where Yancey is standing. Yancey looks her over at some length.*)

Yancey: My, she's so … so … dirty.

Mandy: Listen, my dear. If you'd been where I've been the past few nights, you'd be dirty too. I got thrown out of the shelter three days ago. Had to sleep under a sewer grating near this building. At least it was kind of warm there, and no one bothered me.

Ned (*sniffs the air*): Sewer, eh? I never would have guessed.

Mandy: Well, let's get it over with, officer. Isn't it time to be calling the police?

Ned: Say, just what are you doing here, anyway? There's not supposed to be anyone in the store after hours. How did you get in here?

Mandy: Get in? I walked in with all the rest of the people, this afternoon. It's so nice and clean and warm in here. When no one was looking, I snuck into the manger scene behind the figures and kind of covered myself with straw. No one saw me. I thought I'd at least have a warm, safe place to stay over Chr … over the holiday.

Yancey: You were going to spend your Christmas huddled in a dark department store in the straw in some manger scene? You were going to spend your Christmas here? In this place? What kind of a thing is that to do?

Mandy: Listen, lady. I heard you talking. What's the difference between my spending the night in the manger scene there and you spending your time bent over that desk? Both of us are alone. Both of us have nowhere to go. Both of us are extras no one is thinking about. Isn't that right?

Yancey *(defensively):* But I have a home. I have a place to stay. I have my own place.

Mandy: Yeah, and a cat and a can of soup for Christmas Eve. Let's face it, my dear. We're both on the short end of the Christmas thing. We both have no one … no one.

Yancey: Well, I never! I'm not like you …

Mandy: I hope you never have to be like me. I hope you never have to live like I do. I've got nothing anymore. They took it all away, those people who said they'd take care of my money for me. And when there was no money left, I had no place to go. I live from day to day now. No one cares.

Yancey: How terrible.

Mandy: Yeah, terrible all right. And you know what's the most terrible? The memories. Memories of what used to be. *(Quieter.)* I remember the glow of Christmas at my parents' house and my own children gathered around me. I remember singing and the laughter. My heart can still hear the laughter. *(Pause.)* But I can hardly see the faces anymore.

Ned: Listen, that's real sad and all. But you can't be hanging around in here.

Mandy: I know. I know. I have to go. I have to move on. No room for you here, old lady. No place for you here. You'll just have to move out with the rest of the trash, the rest of the garbage. Maybe you can find something soft behind the building where they throw out the cardboard and the old boxes. Maybe you can find some packing material to lie on. No room for you here.

Ned: Come on. That's not what I'm saying. I'm just saying that you can't stay here. We can't be putting up every …

Mandy: Every what? Every homeless bum? Every worthless piece of baggage? Every useless, empty pile of clothing that happens to be breathing? Is that what you were going to say?

Ned: No. I didn't mean that. I just meant that you'll have to find shelter somewhere else. I can't be responsible for you here. You might get hurt or lost.

Mandy *(laughs):* Do you know how funny that is? Can you hear what you are saying? You are telling me that I might get hurt or lost. *(Emphaticly.)* My dear sir—I am hurt! I am lost!

Ned: But I don't know what I can do for you.

Mandy: It's all right, son. I know. I know all about the excuses and what has to be done. I've heard them all a thousand times. You know, it's funny. I kind of thought that I might find room in the stable there, even though it's a phoney. Doesn't the stable story have something to do with making room?

Yancey *(reflecting):* "And she gave birth to her firstborn, a son. She wrapped him in cloths and placed him in a manger, because there was no room for them in the inn."

(Ned goes over and takes Mandy by the arm.)

Ned: Come on now. I'll show you where the door is. I hate to do this, but …

Mandy: There's no room in the inn, right, officer? There's no room in this place for an old, empty piece of baggage like me.

Ned: Come on.

(Yancey goes over and takes Mandy by the arm and pulls her away from Ned).)

Yancey: Leave her be, Ned. You don't have to throw her out.

Ned: But she can't stay here. You know that.

Yancey: I know. She's coming to my house with me. Mathilda is waiting for us.

(Ned pulls Yancey aside.)

Ned: I don't know. What do you know about this person? How do you know it's safe? And besides, she's so dirty. Do you really want her in your apartment?

Yancey: I know I'm taking a chance. But I have to.

Ned: Why? You don't have to do anything. The old woman can find shelter somewhere.

Yancey: Somewhere like in an old stable, Ned?

Ned: No, I mean like in a shelter.

Yancey: Ned, I can't let her go. I can't send her away. A while ago I prayed for the Christ Child to come and be with me. I think he's come.

Ned: Come on, Mrs. Yancey. Are you saying that God sent this old bag lady to you? That's pretty hard to believe.

Yancey: I don't know, Ned. I don't know what I'm saying. But I know I can't send her away. I look in her eyes, and I see myself there. I see myself in a few years … wandering … *(Pause.)* I can't leave her alone.

Ned: Well, it's too much for me. You do what you want to. But don't say I didn't warn you.

(Yancey goes up to Mandy.)

Yancey: I want you to come with me. To my house. I want you to spend Christmas with me. I've got a little turkey to roast and even some cranberries. Will you come?

Mandy: I don't get it. I thought you didn't want me around.

Yancey: Like you said, we're both alone. We might as well be alone together. You would be doing me an honor if you would come.

Mandy: Sure. Sure I'll come. I honestly don't have anything else on my schedule.

Yancey: Good. Wait till I get my coat.

(Yancey goes off.)

Mandy *(to Ned):* You know. I think it works.

Ned: What's that?

Mandy: When I was there in the stable, I pretended I was a little child again, and I said a prayer like I used to at my bedside. I asked God to send someone for me—tonight—so I wouldn't have to be alone on Christmas. I guess it works.

(Yancey returns in her coat, and the two go off together, arm in arm. Ned goes over and peers at the manger scene.)

Ned: Well, I'll be switched. I guess it does work.

Homily: Gift Giving/Joy Giving

Text: For the wages of sin is death, but the gift of God is eternal life in Christ Jesus our Lord. *Rom. 6:23*

Engaging the Listener

Let's face it, Christmas has become something of a chore. We end up doing a lot of things because they are expected—even though we often do not feel like doing them at all. We put up decorations—often not because we want to, but because it is expected. And we invite people to the house—often not because we particularly want to have them at our house, but because we "owe" them an invitation.

And even in gift-giving, we often find ourselves trudging through stores, racking our brains, and breaking our budgets to get gifts, not so much because we want to give the gift, but because it is expected, and we would feel foolish if we received a gift from someone and did not have something to give in return.

That kind of gift-giving is really quite a chore. We have to be sure that the gift is expensive enough (we don't want to look cheap) and yet not too expensive (we don't want to appear pretentious). The gift has to fit, appear to be carefully chosen, and meet the receiver's expectations. The whole thing is pretty complicated. And pretty joyless.

Exploring Our Need

We have probably done the same thing to all of Christmas. We have made it into a little exercise in living out our expectations. The trouble is, almost everything we do that carries with it great expectations disappoints us.

How often haven't we heard: "Thank goodness Christmas is over, and we can get back to normal." Or something similar—even on our own lips?

What happened? What have we done to the celebration of the coming of the Christ Child? What have we done to the song of the angels and the joyful exuberance of the shepherds? Have we buried them all in expectations and exchanges and grudging activities? No wonder Christmas fails to excite us, fails to give us joy or peace.

Applying the Good News

Fortunately, God does not act that way. God is not busy hurrying about heaven trying to find just the right gift for us—one that we want, one that will fit our expectations, one that we think will fulfill our joy. God is not in the gift-exchange business. God does not give the expected gift in the expected way at the expected time. God gives perfect gifts because they are gifts given out of love to fit our needs and not our wants. God's gifts meet our brokenness and not our expectations. God's gift of the Christ Child meets all of our needs with God's healing presence and power—not because we expect it, but because we need it.

And, interestingly, we will never find the real joy of Christmas until we join God in giving out of love, unexpectedly, to meet needs and not expectations.

Many people rail against Santa Claus as a "pagan god." Perhaps he has become that. Many oppose Santa because he focuses children's attention in the wrong place, makes Christmas giving a kind of payback system, and confuses children's minds with myths that pretend to be real. Perhaps all of that is true.

But very likely Santa (and related figures) probably began as a way for parents to find the joy of giving. Gifts that parents give to children "because they are expected to" don't bring much joy. Gifts that the children "earn" by being good bring joy to neither the giver nor the receiver. Gifts that are given in order to "bribe" children to do better in the future don't have much happiness in them. But what if parents could give gifts that would be sudden and surprising, expecting no payback, given freely out of a spirit of love, without any strings attached? In that kind of giving, parents begin to discover the real joy of Christmas giving, the real joy of reflecting God's gift to us.

Whether or not we buy into Santa Claus, if we want to recapture the joy of Christmas and respond to the gift of God in the Christ Child in a way that will open Christmas for us to the joy and peace that it can have for us, we will want to find ways to really give this Christmas.

That means giving out of love, expecting nothing in return, not giving as a reward, not asking for any recognition or praise for the gift. It means giving gifts that reflect the undeserved and unconditional love that God has for us—like Mrs. Yancey's unexpected gift in the play.

Here is an Advent/Christmas challenge for each of us. In the midst of the doing and the expectations and the buying of gifts that are not really gifts at all, how can we find the joy of giving again—giving freely, as God has given to us, reflecting the gift of Christ to us?

How can we find again, the joy of giving as we receive God's immeasurable gift?

Amen.

Questions/Activities for Reflection/Discussion

1. "Christmas has become too routine, too expected." Agree? Disagree? How is that statement true for you? For your family? How does it show itself in what you do at Christmas? What can you do to take the expectations out of Christmas and find new joy together?

2. Reflect on or tell about a time when you gave a gift that really brought you joy. What was that gift? Why was it given? What made it special? What did it have to do with God's giving?

3. "The family that finds joy knows how to give in love." Agree? How does that show itself in the life of families that you know? In your family? What happens when love is not given? What healing can we find in God's gifts to us?

4. Some have pointed out that worship services are really celebrations of God's gifts. How is that true for you? What gifts do you receive and celebrate in worship? What gifts come to you through Word and Sacrament? How can you share those gifts with others?

5. **Family/Intergenerational:** Make or purchase a gift and give it as a complete surprise to someone in your neighborhood or congregation. Give it to someone who would least expect it and make it clear that you want nothing in return. What is the result of your gift? What does the giving do for you? For the recipient? How does your gift reflect God's gift to us?

The Coming

An Advent/
Christmas drama
in two scenes

Characters

Hal—*middle-aged
man, casual dress*

Alice—*middle-aged
woman, casual
appearance, Hal's
wife*

Clown—*male—
baggy pants, white
face—a large painted
smile and large tears*

Emma—*clown's
wife—young woman
ready to give birth*

Scene 1

Scene suggests the living room of a modest house—with a central couch or chair and a chair off toward a corner. There's a card table without chairs set near the center of the stage. A large box of Christmas decorations sits nearby. It is evening. The stage is dimly lit. Some Christmas decorations are scattered around. A sound system might convey the sound of wind outside.

Hal and Alice silently go about decorating a small, artificial Christmas tree. They don't seem to have much enthusiasm for the project.

Hal: What time did Marge say that she and the others would be here tomorrow?

Alice *(listlessly):* I think about one.

Hal: I guess we let this decorating go long enough. I don't think I've ever put up Christmas decorations on Christmas Eve before. *(He tries to laugh a little.)* But we need to get something up. The children will expect something.

(Alice remains silent as she reaches into the box and brings out a stable for a crèche display. She places it carefully on the table, stops and turns away.)

Alice: I don't want to put this up. Jimmy always did this. He always put this up …

(She slumps on the couch. Hal comes over, kneels in front of her, and takes her gently by the shoulders.)

Hal: Come on. We agreed to try to get hold of ourselves. I know you're hurting, but it's been four months now. I know you loved him, but we can't grieve forever.

Alice: But none of this seems to matter. It's all so meaningless now. Every decoration mocks me. Every ornament reminds me. *(Pause.)* It's just too much …

(She puts her head in her hands. Hal stands over her.)

Hal: Well, we have no choice about this. We have to do it for the others—for the children. They'll expect a Christmas celebration that is at least passably joyful. We can't have them come and just mope around all day.

Alice: Oh, it's so easy for you to talk, to mock me too. After all, Jimmy was only your stepson. I don't think you ever even really cared for him. (*Angry.*) Oh, how can you be so callous, so unfeeling?

(*He turns away.*)

Hal: Now you're not being fair. How can you say I didn't care? I treated that boy like my own child. I gave him everything.

(*She's lost in her own grief, not really listening to him.*)

Alice: It's so unfair. How could it have happened? First, Fred—I lost him when Jimmy was so little. And now Jimmy. He was so happy and full of life one minute, and then the next … (*Pause.*)

You know, sometimes—it's so strange. I come into the room, and it's almost as if I can feel him sitting there in that chair where he always sat. I can almost hear the rattle of the magazine pages or hear his voice … It's so real sometimes. I think I might be losing my mind.

(*She covers her face with her hands again. He approaches, standing over her.*)

Hal: You've got to get hold of yourself. It's over. You can't keep living in the past. You've got to go on. Feeling sorry for yourself is going to get you nothing but more pain.

(*She stands now to confront him angrily.*)

Alice: If I don't have a right to feel sorry for myself, who does? I've lost a husband and an only son. What else do I have to put up with? Oh—it's so easy for you to talk. You are so in control about everything. Well, I'm hurting, and I don't know what to do! I'm in real pain, and there's no way out! (*She sits again—long pause.*) I can still see him there—in that cold box. And I think of him lying there alone … I want to go to him and hold him again like I used to. How could God have let this happen? How could God have done this?

(*He's still looming over her.*)

Hal: It wasn't God driving that car. It was that drunk, that miserable … (*at a loss for words*).

Alice: Do you think that helps? Do you think it helps to know who is to blame? I don't know who's at fault. I don't care. I just know I'm hurting.

(*He's a little gentler now. He touches her on the shoulder.*)

Hal: Well, we have to get ready. Let's just try to forget it. Let's try to make the best of Christmas …

(*She stands again. She is very angry now.*)

Alice: Make the best of it? You make the best of it! I just want to be left alone! I don't want anyone near me! I don't want to have to put on a Christmas face and pretend! I don't want to have to talk about him. I don't want any of it! (*She throws some of the decorations.*) Just take all of this—all of this phoney Christmas stuff—and get it out of here! And you go with it …

(*She turns away from him. He reaches to her but doesn't seem to know what to do.*

The doorbell rings. She keeps her back turned, so finally he goes to answer it.

There in the real or imagined doorway is a clown in costume. Hal stands there for a beat or two, trying to make sense out of it.)

Alice (*impatiently*): Well, who is it?

Hal: It's a clown.

Alice: What? What did you say?

Hal: I said … it's a clown.

(*She turns and comes over to see.*)

Clown (*buoyantly, almost giddy*): Listen. I'm sorry, but I've got a problem. I was on my way to do a benefit for some children—Christmas Eve, you know—over at the hospital, but my car broke down. Not much of a car, don't you know. (*He laughs a little.*) But with it being Christmas Eve and snowing so hard and all, well, I just can't seem to find anyone to help.

(*Hal and Alice stare at him dumbfounded. Finally, he gestures as if calling on the phone. They look at each other.*)

Hal (*startled*): Oh … I guess you can come in and use the phone, if you want to …

(*Clown enters house as he speaks. Hal and Alice back away.*)

Clown: Oh—thanks. I hope I can find something open. You see, it's just that my wife … she's in the car. She's pretty near her time, and I'd like to make her comfortable …

Alice *(incredulous):* Near her time? Do you mean she's going to have a baby?

Clown *(chuckles):* Yeah. Pretty soon. Our first. *(He grins.)* But I don't think right away. I took her along with me, though, so I could kind of keep an eye on things. And now this.

(Hal pulls him aside.)

Hal: But wait! You can't bring a woman who is about to have a baby in here. What would we do with her, for her? My wife and I aren't up to …

(Clown, smiling all the time, tries to calm him.)

Clown: Please, sir—we won't be any trouble. We tried a couple of houses already—with no luck. Some of those over there—the people weren't home. Another had a big party and didn't want to be bothered. We'll try to be quiet, and I'll try to get hold of someone to get us going again. You know. I'll just run out and get Emma. She's not very big and won't take up much space …

(He exits. Hal and Alice watch the door. Hal looks over at her and kind of shrugs. She makes protesting sounds. The two come back. Clown is guiding his wife, arm around her waist. He leads her to a chair in the corner of the room—the one Alice indicated was Jimmy's chair—and helps her sit down. She sits quietly.

Clown makes the phone gesture again. Hal points to the phone on the other side of the room. As the clown goes to make a call, Alice approaches the woman carefully and stares at her, saying nothing. Hal sits on the couch and waits. Clown tries several calls. Nothing …)

Clown *(chuckles):* I can't seem to get anything. I got one to ring. But now nothing. Not even a dial tone. I guess some of the lines are down.

(As Alice watches, woman in the corner has what appears to be a labor pain. Alice turns away, horrified.)

Alice *(to Hal and Clown):* That woman is in labor. She should be in a hospital. She can't have that baby here. I can't take it. I can't do it.

Clown: Isn't that just like a baby? Always coming when you least expect it.

(Alice turns on him and confronts him.)

Alice: How can you be so happy? Are you crazy bringing a woman about to give birth out on a night like this? What is the matter with you? Your wife is in labor, and you're carting her all over creation in a broken-down car. Have you no brains, no feeling? Nothing!

Clown *(smiling):* Nothing, but God.

Alice: God! Where is God in this? Did God send you out on a night like this? Did God break down your car and put you in danger? Did God bring you to this door?

Clown: No. *(He chuckles again.)* I guess I did most of that all by myself. But it doesn't matter. Don't you know that God cares for fools and clowns and little children? I don't know how, but I know God will be with us.

Alice *(scornful):* God will take care, and everything will work out all right. Is that it? *(She turns.)* Give me a break! I've heard that before. *(She is furious with him.)* Why didn't you plan for this? Why didn't you make some arrangements? You can't just come in on people and expect us to bail you out!

Clown *(still smiling):* I don't expect anything. But I am grateful.

Alice: Listen, there is no room for you here. We've got troubles of our own. We've got our own pain to deal with. *(She almost shouts.)* Don't you understand, we don't have a place for you or for your wife or for your baby? We don't have any room …

(Alice sits on the couch and begins to weep. Clown goes into a pantomime. He comes and takes her hand and kisses it dramatically. Then he takes her face and pulls it up to look at him; he wipes the tears from her eyes with his fingers. Then he goes to the box still on the table and takes the figurines out one at a time. He tells the Christmas story in pantomime. With the Joseph figure, he seems to be knocking at doors and searching. Finally, finding a place—he makes his imaginary wife comfortable. Clown sets the Joseph and Mary figures carefully in the crèche. Then he takes out the baby. He pantomimes Joseph's surprise and delight in the birth of the baby, wrap-

ping the child and placing it carefully in the manger. Then he fairly jumps for joy as he runs over and takes Alice's hand. He leads her to the manger and by pantomime indicates that the gift is for her. He takes the baby and places it gently in her hand, touching the tears from her cheeks and from his own. Then he helps her place the child back into the manger. Finally, she collapses on him, weeping. He comforts her. After a time, she begins to stop her sobbing and looks at him. He smiles broadly and cradles her face as one does to one who is cherished. Then he leads her over to where Emma is sitting and puts their hands together. Alice leads Emma out of the room.

Darkness or the sound of a clock ticking indicates the passage of time.

Clown and Hal wait. Clown makes a mime out of pacing and worrying, looking at his watch, fidgeting, looking at the clock. Then, he sits next to Hal. They join hands and bow their heads in prayer. Finally, offstage—the cry of a baby. The clown leaps and dances for joy.)

Scene 2

Same living room—morning.

Hal is in the room, dressed up now. He's kind of fussing with the decorations. Alice enters.

Alice: Merry Christmas, dear.

(She goes over and kisses him quickly.)

Hal: Merry Christmas. *(He points.)* Look. It stopped snowing. I guess Marge and the children may make it after all.

(Alice doesn't answer. She goes over and runs her hand over the manger scene, touching each of the figures. Hal goes to the tree, takes a package from it, and brings it to her.)

Hal: Here, hon. This is for you. Because I love you.

(She seems a little flustered, then goes to a corner and picks up a brown paper bag. She places it in his hands.)

Alice: And this is for you. *(She's a little embarrassed.)* I'm sorry. I didn't have time to wrap it. *(Pause.)* No. That's not true. I didn't wrap it because I didn't feel like wrapping gifts. At least until … *(She pauses, shakes her head,* *and turns away from him.)* Come on, we've got to be ready. Marge and the children will be here soon, and I've got all those gifts to wrap.

Hal *(catching her by the arm):* Do you want to?

Alice: Yes, sure. I guess so. We should. For their sakes.

Hal: And for ours?

Alice: Yes, and for ours. *(Pause.)* Did it really happen? Did it happen the way I remember last night? Did the clown come and make us smile? And was a baby born in our bedroom—born right into my hands? Did that really happen?

Hal: Yes, the clown came and surprised us both. And the baby came too, even though we weren't ready for that either.

Alice: Weren't we? Maybe we were ready. Maybe we were more ready than we knew.

Hal: Maybe.

Alice: Hal, I think he knew. I think the clown knew about Jimmy and my pain. He seemed to know.

Hal: How could he know? We never saw him before.

Alice: He seemed to feel what I was feeling. He seemed to be able to touch my heart and share my hurt and my grief with me. It was like he brought something with him … like a—I don't know—like …

Hal: A gift?

(She goes over to the manger scene and touches the figures.)

Alice: Yes. Like a gift.

Hal: Maybe he did know. Perhaps somehow he could feel …

Alice: Or maybe someone knew we needed him to come. *(Pause.)* I guess what the clown said is true. It must be true.

Hal: What was that?

(She goes over and puts her arms around him.)

Alice: God does care for fools and clowns—and even for lost little children like you and me. *(She kisses him.)* Merry Christmas, my dear. Oh, Hal, a very blessed, foolish, loving Christmas to both of us.

Homily: He Still Comes to Stables

Text: [God sent His Son] to redeem those under law, that we might receive the full rights of sons. *Gal. 4:5*

Engaging the Listener

We had a minor disaster a couple of years ago during our usual preparations for Christmas. The dog ate the manger scene. Well, he didn't exactly eat it. But somehow, as we were busy putting up the tree, he got into the box with the manger-scene figures—all made out of painted papier-maché—and chewed up a couple of them. We were left with a headless Joseph, a shepherd without a left leg, and two fragmented wise men.

We went out and bought a new set of figures—ceramic, I might add. We could have glued together the chewed ones, but somehow that would not have seemed right. If there is one thing that the manger scene needs to be, it is right. It has to look right. The figures have to be in the right places, everything carefully arranged.

Like the other decorating that we do for Christmas, there is a sense about it that we have to do things in the right way, put things in the right places—partly because the ritual of decorating helps us remember, but partly because we have this back-of-the-mind sense that if we don't decorate right, Christmas will not be right.

Exploring Our Need

It is as if there is this perfect Christmas out there. It is made up of our memories, our hopes, our dreams. In this perfect Christmas, everything works just right; everyone is happy; everyone gets the right gifts; everything happens on time. And as a result, we will find ourselves (we hope) strangely healed and warmed as we are made right and filled with the Christmas spirit. We search for that sense of joy and awe and fulfillment we found as a child when we discovered the gifts under the tree on Christmas morning and wallowed in the getting and the loving that it all represented.

But perfect Christmases have long since escaped us. Oh, Christmas is all right. When we get things in the right order and when we do things in the right way and when we gather the right people and when the right gifts get given—Christmas is good to us. But it is never perfect. Little failures, disappointments, and mistakes haunt every celebration and sometimes turn our laughter into tears, even when we don't want it to happen.

Applying the Good News

Just think what it would have meant if God had waited to send Jesus into the world until the world got it right. Suppose God waited until everything was in the right place and the expectations were perfected and the place of his arrival was properly arranged. How long would we have waited for the coming of the Christ Child?

And if we wait for the fullness of Christmas until we "get it right," Christmas will never be anything more for us than a passing moment of near joy in the midst of the whirl of days.

"When the time had fully come," the text says. That time is God's time. And God continues to send the Christ Child into our world, our homes, and our hearts in his time—not ours. God sends Jesus into the world, not because the world is ready, but because the world needs him to come.

In the play, no one was ready for the birth of the child. In fact, the home and the hearts of the characters seemed to be most unready. And yet the gift came, and healing came, and renewal came—when they least expected it, but when they most needed it.

God sends the joy, the gift of Christmas into

our lives, not because we make things properly ready, but because he continues to come where we need him to come. Like a caroling choir of angels on the Palestine hills; like the birth of a gift child in a dirty, animal-smelling stall—he comes. To the places where we need him to come. To our loneliness, our brokenness, to our grief, our pain.

To the stable places in our hearts, he comes. To the stable places in our homes. To the places where we cannot even face our own need—that's where he comes.

In the fullness of this time, in God's time, God sends his son—not to the perfection of Christmas preparations, but to us, to our broken, painful, incomplete hearts and lives. That's where he comes.

Thank God, in the fullness of God's time, Jesus still comes to stables with the gift of life and light.

Amen.

Questions/Activities for Reflection/Discussion

1. Reflect on or share a time when a Christmas blessing arrived in an unexpected and needed way. What happened? What gift was given? How was that gift shared? How was God's gift of the Christ Child involved in that gift?

2. Reflect on or share a time when a Christmas for you was a disappointment or came at a bad time or failed to bring you joy. What caused that failure? How did God reach you in spite of that difficulty? Who brought you God's gifts? What did you learn from that broken Christmas about God? about yourself? about others?

3. God often acts in surprising ways to meet people's needs. How did Jesus meet the needs of people in surprising ways in these accounts: Luke 5:17–25; Matt. 14:22–32; Matt. 19:13–15; John 4:3–41; John 8:3–11? What other Biblical events show how God meets needs in surprising ways? Share some of these. What do all of these tell us about God's love for us, about God's giving, about God's grace?

4. "Jesus still comes to stables." How has that saying been true for you? What stables in your life or in your home need him to come this year? What will his coming do? How will you celebrate that coming? How will you share it with others?

5. **Family/Intergenerational:** Work out a new way to tell the Christmas story to each other or to others. What way can you tell the story using the manger scene in your home? What can you make or create that would help you tell the story? What display might you use? Create a family ritual around putting up the manger scene that includes telling the Christmas story in words and actions and prayers for the Christ Child to come to your hearts and homes. How can you share your story?

Family Themes
Six Dramas

Introduction

In 1984, the University of Nebraska did research on the characteristics of "strong" families. They were able to identify six elements or features that are common to strong, enduring families: commitment, spiritual wellness, appreciation, communication, coping with crisis, and time together. These characteristics were explained in a book published by Berkley Books, New York, in 1986: *Secrets of Strong Families*. The six dramas to follow each focus on one of these characteristics. Homilies (with discussion questions) are included after each drama.

Using These Dramas

These dramas are intended for use in worship. They could be part of a series of six worship experiences (e.g., for Lent) which focus on these six characteristics of healthy families and apply them both to families in the congregation and to the congregation itself. The dramas have these features in common:

- They require few "actors" and little rehearsal. The parts can be read, if time to memorize is not available.

- They require little scenery (only enough to "set the stage") and minimal costuming.

- Most of the parts can be adapted to men or women. Young people (with a little makeup when they need to look older) enjoy doing dramas like these.

- They can all be done in a worship setting. Since they require minimal "space," performing the dramas in a chancel area would work well.

The dramas can also be performed at a congregational "family night" or in other gatherings. Whether used in worship or another setting, the dramas are intended to "open the subject" and help people think about and begin to relate the characteristic featured to their own lives. The dramas can be followed by one of the following:

- A time of silent reflection.

- A time of small group discussion (questions for discussion are included).

- A time of family interaction (an intergenerational activity is suggested for each drama). In a congregational setting, these intergenerational activities can be done by small groups (groups of five or six that include people of varying ages).

- The homily included in this resource or another.

- An open discussion time that includes a panel presentation or debate.

These resources also could form the core of activities at a "family enrichment" retreat done in the church building or away. Each of the dramas, followed by the homily and a time of family discussion and interaction, could form six "learning sessions" at an overnight retreat or an all-day enrichment workshop for families. A retreat-type setting would provide ample time for families to do the family activity suggested with each drama.

About Staging

Each of these dramas suggests a specific setting. Some of the settings (for example, the "kitchen" in the drama *Commitment*) are important to the drama itself. But none of the settings are elaborate. In a worship area, the setting for the drama can be simply suggested with a few props. A couch indicates a living room. A table suggests a kitchen. Since the dramas all turn on the relationship of the characters, the setting is only background. Audiences will quickly focus on the characters. At that point, the setting becomes irrelevant. For that reason, you will want to keep your staging and the props you use as simple as possible.

Characters

Father—*about 40, "at home" clothing*

Mother—*about 40, comfortable clothing*

Daughter—*teenage, typical teen attire*

Son—*teenage, casual clothing*

Appreciation

Scene

The stage area—with a couch and TV—suggests a living room. In the center of the stage is a scraggly Christmas tree.

Father, taking ornaments out of a large box, is decorating the tree. Mother stands nearby watching. Daughter is on the couch watching TV.

Father *(aggravated):* Blankety-blankety Christmas tree lights. They're always tangled. Why can't anyone ever put these things away right? Every year it's the same thing.

Mother: Well, you put them away yourself, Mr. Clever. As I recall, you were in such a hurry to get the tree down that you didn't have time to put them away …

Father: Listen, spare me the details. That's all you ever do is nag. I know I'm not perfect. But you're not a walking saint either.

Son *(offstage):* Dad, can I come out of my room now?

Mother: Yeah—I think we'd better let him out. It may be cruel and unusual punishment to keep him in there for more than an hour. The health department may condemn it at any minute.

Father: Sarcastic. Always sarcastic. I suppose you're such an outstanding housekeeper that you are going to give him lessons. Maybe you could start by knitting something with that roll of dust under the table there.

Mother: Complain, complain. That's all I ever get.

Son: Dad! Can I come out?

Father: Okay! Okay! I was just trying to do you a favor. With those grades, a little more time with the books certainly wouldn't break anything in your head. What, are you studying to be the world's dopiest kid?

Daughter *(very loudly):* Can't you people be quiet? Can't you see I'm trying to watch television? Shouting and hollering. That's all we ever get around here.

Father: And I suppose you're not shouting and hollering. Your voice, my dear, has all of the quality of a strangled cat.

Daughter: Just bug off and leave me alone, will you?

Father *(to himself):* Now where is that stupid angel that's supposed to go at the top of this tree? I put it in here *(digs in box)* somewhere. It must be here.

Mother: Why don't you try looking on what you call your workbench—of course, it would probably be April before you could get through all the junk.

Father *(still digging):* It's not here. It's just not here. And I would like to know who took the thing anyway.

Mother: Someone took it just to aggravate you, don't you know? I mean, why should Christmas be any different than any other day? I'm getting a headache.

Father: And I'm getting another pain in the neck. Junior, why don't you find the angel?

Son: Me? I don't know anything about it. If you had your wits about you, you might not lose everything …

(Doorbell rings.)

Son: Get that, will you, Mom?

Mother: Me? I'm way over here. You get it.

Son: Let her get it *(indicates daughter)*. She isn't doing anything but keeping the couch from floating away.

Daughter: Oh, bug off, creep!

Father: I'll get it. You people are such a pain.

(Father goes to door. Audience can't see who is there. There is some mumbling and then Father comes back carrying a tree-ornament angel in his hand. He's kind of dazed. He stands there holding it and staring at it.)

Mother: Well, who was it?

(Silence.)

Mother: Hey, you with the ears, who was at the door?

Father: Huh? Oh, just some delivery boy. He said he had this for us. Isn't it beautiful?

Mother: What?

Father: I said, isn't it beautiful? I mean, it's just like our angel used to be. It reminds me of you, my dear. You were so beautiful …

Mother: What did you say?

Father: What did I say? What made me say that?

Son: Dad, are you feeling all right?

Father: Yes, and it is so nice of you to ask about me, Son. I appreciate the way you take a concern for my health and try to help out …

Son: What? What's the matter with you?

Father: Yeah, what *is* the matter with me?

Daughter: Who sent the delivery boy, anyway?

Father: He didn't say. He just said that this was for us. That we needed it.

Daughter: Needed it? What does that mean?

Father: I'm not sure, but it is typical of you to try to figure it out, Daughter. You are so clever about things like that. I appreciate the insights you offer …

Daughter: What did you say?

Father: What did I say? *(He hands angel to his son.)* Here, my boy, will you use your balance and skill and put this on the tree?

Son *(takes the angel, stares at it for a moment, and then seems to shake a little):* Sure, Dad. I'd be glad to. I've been looking for a way to show you how much I appreciate all you do for us, especially at Christmas. And after I get this on the tree, I'm going to clean my room … *(Pause.)* What am I saying?

Mother: What *are* you saying?

Son: This is strange! I have this great urge to clean up my room and to tell you how much I love you all. I must be sick or something.

Daughter: You must have weirded out again.

Son: Listen, there's something wrong with this thing. Here *(throws ornament on the couch next to his daughter),* you take it.

Daughter *(picking ornament up off the sofa and examining it):* It just looks like any ordinary ornament. But there is a kind of sparkle to it. *(Pause; she trembles.)* Kind of like the sparkle I feel inside when I think of the Christmases we've spent together. Did I ever tell you how much I appreciate all of what you have done to make our holiday celebrations special ... What am I saying?

Mother: There's something wrong with that angel!

Daughter: Wrong? I feel better than I've felt in years.

Father: Me too!

Son: Me too. And I still want to clean my room.

Mother: Give me that thing! *(She grabs the angel and starts offstage, holding it as if to throw it.)* I'll show you what to do with it. Let's put it right here where we can all enjoy it. It is just the thing that this tree needs to make it perfect—as perfect as you always make our trees, dear. *(She kisses her father.)* Have I ever told you how much I appreciate all that you do for ... What's the matter with me?

Father: I don't know, but I feel wonderful. Like Christmas is right now.

Daughter: Like we can celebrate right now?

Mother: I feel like singing.

Son: And cleaning.

Father: I wonder who sent that angel? I wonder who knew how much we needed to have it in our house?

Mother: Yes, I wonder ...

Homily: The Posture of Thanks

Reflection Text: [Give] thanks to God the Father through him [Jesus].
Col. 3:17

Engaging the Listener

- A teacher was reviewing the Lord's Prayer with her students. "What are you thankful for in the prayer?" she asked one of her students. "For the eagles," he said. The teacher was puzzled. "Yeah, you know," he continued, "deliver us from eagles."

- A speaker harangued against the evils of higher education—against universities and students and all the liberal ideas that were dispensed there. "I'm thankful," he said, "that I never went to one of those wicked places and got my mind all messed up."

  The next speaker was a learned professor. "Do I understand you to say that you are thankful for your ignorance?"

  "Yes, you might put it that way," said the other.

  "Then, indeed," said the professor, "you have a great deal to be thankful for."

And so do we all. It would not be difficult to make a long list of things we "ought to be thankful for." We could start with this country, with the many blessings we enjoy, with talents and abilities, with things we own—and on and on.

And it is not difficult, on certain occasions, to say thank you to God. "Thank you, God, for all the good graces we receive," starts lots of the prayers we hear. And certainly, there is nothing wrong with giving thanks to God—even though it is done all too often in a kind of off-hand manner.

Exploring Our Need

But giving thanks is not something that should be reserved for Sunday morning and passing prayers at the dinner table. Giving thanks is a style of living.

Of course, in a sense, saying thank you is easy. We say thanks to the butcher and the grocer and the guy who carries the bags at the airport. We say thanks to the cabbie and the clerk and the kid who delivers the paper. How easy it is, out there where it doesn't mean much, to say thanks.

How difficult it often is at home. How often do we hear it? Honestly now. How often do we hear (on our own tongue), "Thanks, for what you have done for me today, for cooking and cleaning and minding the house. Thanks for taking the garbage out and cutting the grass."

And as rarely as those are heard, how often do we hear (or speak) even more important words like these: "Thank you for being there today, for staying with me, for knowing me well enough to hate me and loving me still. Thanks for not giving up on me, for being patient with me, for loving me at my most unlovable. Thanks for being God's presence to me."

Saying thanks is not just an action. It is not a formula of words that we toss off when we happen to think of it. Giving thanks is a posture, an attitude, a way of relating to others.

A posture of thankfulness is one of the characteristics (one of the secrets) of a family (marriage) relationship with a healthy spirit.

A family with a healthy spirit? What do we mean, spirit?

Have you ever watched a couple in a restaurant, perhaps? You watch a while, and somehow you can sense, even though you can't hear them, the nature of the spirit of their relationship. It may be conveyed by their body posture, the way they look or don't look at each other. In a short time you can "feel" the spirit of that marriage. You can sense the spirit or the personality.

A spirit or personality is the heart of our family

relationships. The spirit is made up of all of what we are, have been, and hope to be. Our attitudes, values, hopes, dreams, commitments—all of these.

In many cases (like too many couples we see in restaurants) the spirit is not well. Sometimes you can actually feel the pain that exists between the two people. Sometimes the spirit has an aura of sadness that is inescapable.

And it happens in our families too. The spirit that we cultivate together is not always well. Sometimes the hurts show up. Sometimes the barriers get too high. Sometimes the pain that we have caused each other comes back to haunt us. The spirit of our family seems to be wounded, sick—and often we seem to be unable to make it well again.

Applying the Good News

If this were a classic "self-help" lecture, I would tell you that I have 18 easy exercises you can do to make the spirit better in your home. But that's not going to happen. The heart of a family does not get better by some trick program or a set of 18 steps.

Nor does the spirit of a congregation. We know that the spirit of a community grows by the power of the Gospel.

You can get activity by scolding or laying down the law.

You can get people busy with programs.

You can give the appearance of life with lots going on, but if the heart of the congregation is not centered in the Gospel of Jesus Christ and the Spirit of life and hope and peace that comes though him, it is all wasted.

Similarly in a family. All of us have, at times, had family spirits that are in various states of disarray. Some families may be seriously troubled. Some may have hurts and wounds. Some may have forgotten how to speak to one another. Some may have angers and fears and frustrations that are putting the spirit to death. In some, the spirit may be virtually dead.

The Gospel says that they may come alive again. The "magic" in the ornament in the drama is the Good News of God's love that comes on Christmas and is perfected on Good Friday and is sent into our lives on Easter Sunday.

Here is the real truth. God does not give up on us. God knows that for all of our good efforts and our doing and busyness, we cannot create life and peace and hope and joy. These are gifts, and God insists on giving them to us. The "fruit of the Spirit is love, joy, peace, patience, kindness, goodness, faithfulness, gentleness, and self-control" (Gal. 5:22–23).

So how important is it to express appreciation—so that "whatever [we] do whether in word or deed," we do it "in the name of the Lord Jesus, giving thanks to God the Father through him" (Col. 3:17)?

It's important because our words, our actions, create reality. The Spirit comes to us and recreates the spirit of our families—a spirit that has its heart in a posture of thankfulness to God and one another.

These things we can do right now, with the Spirit's help, to renew that posture of thankfulness:

1. Set realistic goals for ourselves.

2. Expect success—lean into the future.

3. Cherish one another—faults, failings, and all.

4. Intentionally renew the family relationship.

5. Take time for spiritual renewal together in home devotions and in worship.

6. Live forgiveness daily.

And "whatever [we] do, whether in word or deed," we will do "in the name of the Lord Jesus."

Questions/Activities for Reflection/Discussion

1. Reflect on (share) your family traditions for Thanksgiving Day. What do you do? Why? What "thankfulness" do you find in what you do? Why is Thanksgiving important? Why is it not enough?

2. Look up the words *thanks* and *thanksgiving* in a Bible dictionary or concordance. Read some of the texts cited. What can you learn about giving thanks from the passages? What is the best way to "give thanks."

3. Read together Luke 17:11–19. What can you learn about giving thanks? In what way is giving thanks always a response?

4. Describe the "spirit" of your family or congregation. What is healthy about it? What is unhealthy? How can the renewal God promises in Jesus help you with your family spirit?

5. **Family/Intergenerational:** Write out a number of brief thank you cards—adults can help children. Use 3 × 5 cards. On the front, put a Bible text about giving thanks—like Col. 3:17. On the back, write a short, sincere thank you message. Each person should sign the cards he or she keeps. At home, over the next week, give one of the cards to a family member each time you want to express your thanks. When you have used up your cards, speak the thanks orally. At the end of the week, meet and talk about what it meant to express your thanks to one another.

Commitment

Characters

Grandpa—*about 80, feeble, in slippers and bathrobe*

Jason—*about 30, wearing a business suit*

Scene

The stage area is almost bare—a few props might suggest a kitchen. In the center of the stage area is an old, square, wooden table. There are three chairs at the table.

Grandpa enters and putters in the kitchen, getting ready his small supper.

He sets his tiny pots on the table. Then he uncovers two neat place settings—similar to the way one might uncover the communionware on the altar. He sits in one of the chairs, lays his hands palms up on the table, and prays silently. He begins to eat by himself.

Jason enters rather briskly.

Jason: Grandpa. I didn't know if you'd be home. I thought I'd stop by and see …

Grandpa: My boy—you know I'm always here. Just here …

(Jason crosses to the old man and hugs him awkwardly by the shoulders.)

Jason: Well, you must have been expecting me. I see you set a place for me.

Grandpa: You can sit over here *(indicates other side of table)*.

Jason: But that place? Who is that for?

Grandpa *(quietly after a pause):* It's for her. My Ellie always sits here.

Jason: Oh, Grandpa, hasn't this gone on long enough? You know Grandma is dead; she's been gone more than a year now. Why do you still pretend?

Grandpa: Pretend? You don't know much about pretending, do you, Son? I'm not pretending. I know Ellie died. I was there when they put her coffin in the ground. *(Pause.)* But it doesn't matter. She's here—still here.

Jason: That's silly, Grandpa. Dead people don't live in houses.

Grandpa *(quietly):* How could she not be here? Her breath fills this house. Her smell. Her whisper in the night. Her hand on mine. She's here. She's a part of me, of this house, of our life. *(He puts his head down now.)* I can't forget.

Jason *(earnestly):* I know you've spent most of your life here, Grandpa, but you know what the family decided. You're getting too old to live here by yourself. You need to go somewhere where they can take care of you.

Grandpa *(with finality):* I can't go. I can't leave.

Jason: You have to, Grandpa. What do you want to stay for? There's nothing here anymore. It's just a big, empty, old house. Look! There's practically nothing left—just that broken-down furniture in the living room … and this old, creaky table.

Grandpa: Is that all you see?

Jason: Grandpa, I know the place means a lot to you. But the house and this stuff in it—it's just things. Look at me. I've been married three times. Lived in a different house with each wife. It's no big deal. A house is a house. A place to live. What matters is you. Your well-being. Your health and your care.

Grandpa *(silent for a time; then reaches over and pulls Ellie's empty chair to himself—as if remembering):* I tried to leave once—back then when I thought there were better places to be, better people to be with. Run-down old house, I thought. Run- down life. Tired and worn. Too old and familiar. What does this old house have? Nothing. Empty. Needs work and care all the time. Who wants it? Who needs it?

And I ran to other houses, sat at other tables, joined others who seemed to welcome me, who seemed to care. *(Pause.)* For a time. *(Pause.)* Until I found myself alone one night. Out on the street. No longer welcome in the fine houses with the tables set by the windows to see the view.

I thought of this table then. This broken-down, square, impress-no-one table—and Ellie sitting here alone.

When I came back that night … when I walked in, she was right here. She sat, bending over her bowl; her tears falling right here. *(His fingers gently rub the spot on the table.)*

But do you know—even after I had been gone, after all I

had done—right here, she had a place set for me. *(He caresses the table thoughtfully.)*

"I've not been faithful to you," I told her.

"I know," she said.

"I've been looking for something else, something better, something more exciting."

"I know," she said.

"Are you home to stay?" she asked me.

"Why would you take me back? Why after all that I've said and done? Why?"

"Because this is your place, here beside me, here at my table. I promised, and I cannot turn away from the promise."

And she never mentioned it again.

(Jason shifts uncomfortably. Grandpa continues, rather softly.)

Grandpa: Then later, when her mind was going—when she used to wander and sometimes wonder where she was or who I was—I would fix her hair the way she liked it and put one of her fancy dresses on her. Then I'd bring her here, to this place at her table. You know, no matter how blank her mind or confused she became—here she would smile at me.

I'd hold her fluttering hand, and we would talk about the days past and the memories.

"I'm such a bother," she would say. "So much trouble to take care of. Why don't you just leave me?"

"Because this is your place," I would say. "Here beside me, at my table. I promised, and I cannot turn away from the promise." *(There is a long pause.)*

This house is old and falling down. The table creaks and doesn't sit straight anymore. My body wastes away. But what Ellie and I built together is not the stone and boards, not the lumber that makes this table, nor even the dust of these bodies that have held us for these years. Our spirits are knit together by love and time and faithfulness, by the hand of God and God's eternal promise.

(Stronger, with passion.) If the house falls, if it burns, if

my life slips away like the evening sun—it doesn't matter, for what we had will last forever. By the hand and mercy of God—it will last forever.

(Jason is quiet now. He is looking down at his shoes. Grandpa gets up from the table and gently puts Ellie's chair back under her place.)

Grandpa: And let me ask you, Mr. Man-So-Wise-about-Selling-and-Buying-Houses-and-Changing-Wives-and-Lives—what do you have that will last? When you come to the time when your life begins to crumble, when the walls won't stand anymore and the darkness cannot be chased by wishes and dreams, what will you have then that has God's forever in it?

What will you have then?

Homily: An Unearthly Love

Reflection Text: By this all men will know that you are my disciples, if you love one another. *John 13:35*

Engaging the Listener

Crushed, broken, having lost all, covered with sores, sitting in the ashes, Job says: "Though he [God] slay me, yet will I hope in him" (Job 13:15).

Having lost her husband and facing a difficult trip to a foreign country and an uncertain future with her mother-in-law, Ruth says: "Don't urge me to leave you or to turn back from you. Where you go I will go and where you stay, I will stay. Your people will be my people and your God my God. Where you die I will die, and there I will be buried" (Ruth 1:16–17a).

Having refused to bow down to the golden statue set up by the king, arrested and threatened with immediate death in a furnace of fire, Shadrach, Meshach, and Abednego said: "O Nebuchadnezzar, we do not need to defend ourselves before you in this matter. If we are thrown into the blazing furnace, the God we serve is able to save us from it, and he will rescue us from your hand, O king. But even if he does not, we want you do know, O king, that we will not serve your gods or worship the image of gold you have set up" (Dan. 3:16–18).

Incredible words all. We stand in awe of the strength, courage, and perseverance of these people. They have in common an unbelievable commitment—a dedication that will not let them abandon their faith, their loved one, their integrity.

The words are reminiscent of Martin Luther's famous stand before council and emperor. When threatened with excommunication and death, Luther said: "Here I stand. I cannot do otherwise … God help me."

Exploring Our Need

Such commitment is hard to find in our day. Though we treasure commitment in the heros of history, legend, and story—we rarely encounter it today. We live in the era of the semi-promise, the conditional commitment, the time of pragmatic perseverance.

A young man was interviewed about cheating in his college career. "Sure, I cheat," he said. "Who doesn't?" And would he do it again? "Sure. I wouldn't hesitate, if it helped me."

A woman, attempting to give reason for the divorce she was seeking, said, "We just don't like each other very much anymore. We don't have any fun."

The investment broker stole millions from his investors, in some cases taking people's life savings. "It's just the way business is done these days. Those who are smart enough take what they can."

Commitment has become conditional. The kind of commitment spoken of by Grandpa in the play is so rare that his words sound almost like fantasy.

A current, more practical, marriage promise might read:

> I take you to be my wife/husband from this day forward until it doesn't seem to work very well anymore, and I pledge you my love as long as you give me the kind of love and support I need; I promise to stay with you as long as it is convenient for us both, and I will be as faithful to you as I can under the circumstances.

Certainly, that kind of commitment is often all too common in religious life as well. Though we don't often say it out loud, we often operate with a kind of conditional commitment to God. "If God is good to me," we seem to say, "I will be faithful to God." And though it is not said, certainly the result of that kind of conditional commitment is evident when we hit the trials and troubles of life. Does this sound familiar:

"How could God do this to me? Am I not one of the good people? Doesn't God care that I at least try to live the life of a disciple? I go to church. I do the right thing—most of the time. Certainly I am better than most of the people I live and work with—and look at them. They go merrily along, and I suffer with this … "

The premise of that tirade (though it certainly is understandable) is a conditional contract with God. If I am good, God, will you not be good to me? If you are good to me, God, I will do my part in living as I am supposed to live.

The problem is, conditional commitments are fragile, undependable, and even destructive.

- We know, for example, that children who grow up in an atmosphere of conditional love (I will love and accept you if you do the right thing) grow up feeling unloved.

- We know that marriage commitments based on pay back never survive. If I am in the marriage for what the other person can give me, it will never be enough.

- We know that families are strong only when the bonds that hold them together are unconditional. How can anyone be good enough to deserve to stay in a family?

- We know that faith that is built on a conditional relationship with God cannot survive. How can I be good enough to earn God's gifts? How can God be good enough to me to earn my love and trust?

Amazingly, in our world of conditional commitment, we know that lasting, fulfilling, satisfying, enriching relationships are only built on unconditional commitment.

And if this were a lecture titled "We Need to Do Better"—we could only appeal to our good intentions or self interest to try harder to give

and live unconditional love and unconditional commitment.

And yet, when we look inside ourselves, when we compare ourselves to the great heros of faith and commitment, when we stand before the mirror of God's expectation of unconditional commitment, we find our own promises, our own commitments fragile, breakable, self-serving, and conditional.

We can't seem to do better on our own. It seems unfair to have to love God even when life hurts us. It seems unfair to have to love a child, even when the child disappoints us. It seems unrealistic to expect that we will continue to love a spouse that has betrayed us or worse. It is not fair, is it? It is not right? Will we not be taken advantage of if we love and give unconditionally? Will we not end up the fool, be left holding the bag, be walked on if we don't put conditions on our love or our commitments?

Well, will we not?

Applying the Good News

The answer, surprisingly, at least from God's point of view, is no. We will not lose if we offer unconditional love and commitment to God and to others. In fact, just the opposite. We will find fulfillment, peace, abundance, and joy in the impossible act of unconditional love.

Impossible? Certainly. In ourselves we don't have the strength to give God an unconditional promise of faith, nor to give our spouse an unconditional promise of faithfulness, nor to give our family unconditional love. Those truly unconditional gifts belong to God. And they are given to us.

"God so loved the world … ," the familiar passage says. God loved so much (without condition) "that he gave his one and only son … " without hook or price or condition—for us. God's grace (the word means unconditional, unearned gifting) comes to us without cost or price or condition.

And God's grace brings to us—not good intentions, not better tries at living or giving unconditionally—but the very Spirit of God who makes his home in our hearts and causes us to "overflow" with God's grace.

"By this all men will know that you are my disciples, if you love one another" (John 13:35).

In this strange, individualistic, me-first, grabbing, taking, greedy world—certainly we will stand out like strange "sore thumbs" if we live the unconditional love that we have been given. We will go against what makes sense to the world. We will appear fools to some and weak to others. We will be out of touch and out of the mainstream.

And yet among all the takers and the grabbers and the winners we will have peace where they cannot find it. We will have security in a world that offers none. We will have hope among a hopeless people. We will have permanence in a world of impermanence. And we will have eternity in a world that cannot think or promise past tomorrow.

And they will see. And know. And perhaps, they will find the one who gives the love that will not let us go—the love that will not let us let him go—or let one another go. "And now these three remain: faith, hope and love. But the greatest of these is love" (1 Cor. 13:13).

Questions/Activities for Reflection/Discussion

1. Think of (tell about) a "hero of faith" you have known. It doesn't have to be someone who was famous—many great persons of faith are nearer and more familiar. Tell about (reflect on) that person's life. What made that person a hero to you? What did his or her place in your life have to do with commitment? with unconditional love? What does the example of that person mean to you?

2. Reflect on and share (if you are willing) a time when your commitment to God or to those you love was too "conditional." What did that feel like? How did you feel about yourself? How does forgiveness help us with our commitments?

3. Read 1 Corinthians 13 aloud. What does the chapter have to do with commitment? How do the words inspire you? How do they accuse you? How does the strength to live up to that ideal come to you?

4. Lifelong commitment between two people is a rare treasure. What do the following have to do with that commitment: respect, trust, perseverance, attention, forgiveness, patience, acceptance, humility. Which seems most important? Why? How is God involved in all of these for you?

5. **Family/Intergenerational:** Work together to rewrite Ruth's promise (Ruth 1:16–17) in words that have meaning for your family. (Make a poster for each family represented in your small group.) Put the promise on a large piece of poster board. Decorate it with other words of promise, Bible verses of promise, or symbols that remind you of God's love or our love for one another. Leave space for family members to sign their names to the poster. Put it up in your home where it can be seen often.

Characters

Dad—*about 40, "at home" clothing*

Mom—*about 40, casual clothing*

Son—*teenager*

Daughter—*teenager*

Communication

Scene

The stage area suggests a living room.

The four family members, Dad, Mom, Son, Daughter, are sitting staring at a blank TV screen. They just sit there for a long time. After quite a while, Son gets up and goes out for a moment and comes back with a drink, sits down, and watches the blank screen. Throughout, all of the characters but the Son speak their lines flatly and slowly, with little emotion.

Son: Dad?

Dad: Yes, Son? What is it?

Son: I hate to mention this, but the TV is broken.

Dad: Yes, we know. It went out last night.

Mom: And we called the repairman right away, but he can't come to fix it until tomorrow.

Daughter: So the TV is broken.

Dad: And there's the whole problem …

Mom: In a nutshell, you might say.

(They sit again watching the blank screen.)

Son: Dad?

Dad: Yes, what is it, Son?

Son: Do you think we could do something else?

Dad: Else? What else? We always watch television in the evening.

Son: Yeah, I know. But that's when the television is working.

Dad: What else did you have in mind?

Son: Do you think we might have a talk?

Mom: Talk? Whatever for?

Daughter: We talked last week. Remember? At supper, during the commercial. You said something about eating some seconds on the meat.

Dad: And I told you that too much meat wasn't good for you. Remember?

Son: But that's not a talk. That's talking.

Mom: Yes, dear. That's right.

Son: Can't we have a talk?

Dad: What would we talk about?

Son: I don't know. About stuff. About our lives. About what's happening with us.

Mom: Yes, by the way. What is happening?

Daughter *(perplexed):* I don't know. The TV is broken.

Dad: Yes, so it is. So you see—that's what's happening.

(They sit quietly again.)

Son: But why don't we just try it? Let's just try to have a talk.

Mom: But won't we miss something? What's on TV tonight?

Son *(walks over to the TV—speaks with some passion):* Nothing! Get it? Nothing is on! It's broken!

Dad *(flustered):* Well, I guess we could try having a talk.

Mom *(fretting):* I don't know. I just don't know. It just seems so strange.

Daughter: What will people think if they come to the house and find us sitting here talking? They might lock us up or something.

Dad: Now! Now! Let's go along with our son. Here, let's sit in a circle and have a talk.

(Everyone turns toward each other. They sit looking at each other. No one says anything.)

Son *(tentatively):* I had a dream the other night. I dreamed I was all alone.

Mom: That's nice, dear.

(Long silence.)

Son: Sometimes I think about what I'm going to do with my life—my plans and hopes and dreams.

Dad: He means like a program schedule, I think.

Mom: Is that what you mean, dear?

Daughter: I think this is creepy.

(Long silence.)

Son *(speaking with feeling):* Sometimes I get so sick and tired of the same old thing all the time. I get so mad about what is going on in the world. I get so heartsick over people who are in need with no one to help them—over people who are hurt by wars and … I worry. I worry about the future. About our future. About what might happen.

(The others look at him as if he is a little daft. They move their chairs a little bit farther from him.)

Dad: Are you feeling any better, Son?

Mom: He'll be all right again when the TV is fixed.

Daughter: This is so weird.

(Son gets up and begins to move off.)

Son: I'm going to bed.

Dad: Okay, Son. Tomorrow the old TV will be running again.

Mom: And we can get back to normal.

Daughter: Won't that be terrific?

Homily: Forgive One Another

Reflection Text: You are the people of God. … You must forgive one another just as the Lord has forgiven you. *Col. 3:12–13 TEV*

Engaging the Listener

This happens all too often at my house: I'm watching the news. My wife likes to see the weather report—it has something to do with how her kindergartners will behave the next day. When the weather comes on, I call to her, and she usually comes and watches for a while. We watch the weather in silence. After it is over, I look over at her and say, "What did he say?" And she looks back at me and replies, "I don't know. What *did* he say?" Does this ever happen at your house?

When the woman of the house left, she called to her "Mr. Mom" husband. "Don't forget to put the clothes in the dryer and take the dog to the vet. When she returned, she went to check on progress. "What in the world is the dog doing in the dryer?" she shouted. "I don't know," replied her blissful husband. "And I don't know what the vet is going to do with all those wet clothes, either."

These are two examples of the importance of communication in the home. For years the experts have been telling us that the families that communicate well have a better chance of being successful—keeping the marriage together and raising reasonably stable children—than the families where communication has broken down.

Think about the little drama we just saw. The family was trying to do communication. Think about or talk to someone next to you about these questions:

- Do you think the family in the drama was a Christian family? Why or why not?

- To what extent are Christian families different in their ability to communicate?

- Should Christian families communicate better? Why or why not?

Exploring Our Need

One thing we know for sure, effective communication in the family is getting more and more difficult. The reasons are many:

- We are used to seeing and not seeing, hearing and not listening. How many times do you sit in front of the TV and wonder what you just saw, or hear a report, or a sermon, or a speech and immediately forget what you heard? We have become expert at shutting out sight and sound.

- To a certain extent, we still suffer from role expectations. Males are supposed to be strong and silent. They take their pain raw. They never cry or show vulnerability. They keep things to themselves—until … well, you know.

- We suffer from overextending ourselves. We simply don't seem to have the time to pay attention to those others that fill our house with us. We take them for granted, rush about doing our own thing, take care of what needs to be done—and almost lose contact with the rest of the family. It is part of our world. An example of this is the couple, living some distance outside a metropolitan area, who decided to "give up their children"—the children were six and four at the time—because they could not pay proper attention to the children and pursue their careers at the same time. Are we too busy?

Beyond these problems, long-term relationships often seem to work against effective communication since the effort it takes to practice healthy communication skills is great. Open communication that nurtures relationships takes intention, attention, and work. Frequently, however, we fail, thus, hurting each other and stacking up one grievance on top of another. Over time these unresolved conflicts severely damage our relationships.

It might help to picture our family life as a house. We do things together (at least watch television together) in the family room. We eat—sometimes—in the kitchen. We each have our private rooms in the house—the place where we attend to our own concerns and interests. There is a formal area for guests, and the like. The house of our family life may be large or small, have many people in it or few, be new or old—but it is there, and it represents our closest relationships.

The problem is, the house keeps getting cluttered up. We have a way of storing up the hurts of the past—the unresolved arguments and old subjects we just can't seem to talk about (money, sex, in-laws). It gets harder and harder to get over the clutter and find each other. And each of us expects the other to take care of the clutter of past mistakes and hurts and disappointments. And when the other fails again to undo the wrong of which he or she is guilty, we add resentment to the pile of clutter as well.

The clutter stops communication. Eventually there is nothing to talk about anymore.

"I don't want to hear about it," we say in word or action. "I don't want to go over that again," we say. We begin to avoid each other, stay on our side of the pile of clutter that separates us. And communication dies—and eventually the relationship dies.

I visited an elderly couple on a farm. They boasted to me (separately) that they had not spoken to each other in four years. Four years! Somehow they kept living in the same house, communicating with grunts and hand signals. And I'm not sure they were even clear about why they were not speaking.

If we don't clean the house periodically, communication will die and so will the relation-ships in that house we call our family.

Applying the Good News

Cleaning the house takes work. It can be very painful. It makes us vulnerable. And we can be hurt. It means talking about our feelings. You can buy lots of books and programs that tell you how to make it happen in your home. Every popular magazine has articles like "Five Easy Ways to Make Your Home Happy" or "Ten Steps to Effective Communication." And certainly those kinds of efforts can help. But they do not cure.

What is the difference between any family and a Christian family? Are we better behaved? Are we nicer? Are we better looking? Are we more intelligent? Perhaps, sometimes, but none of those make any difference.

The difference is that as Christian people we have a way of not just moving the clutter around or hiding it in better places. We have a way of getting rid of it forever. It's called for-giveness.

Some years ago, there was a line in a popular movie that caused some stir. It said, "Love is never having to say you're sorry." Well, in the best of all worlds, maybe that would be true. But in the world of brokenness—broken dreams, intentions, resolutions, hearts, and lives—we have to say we are sorry lots of times.

The Christian would change the statement to, "Love is always having to say you're forgiven." Forgiveness is tough stuff. It is both difficult to do and made of God's lasting power.

Forgiveness is not saying, "I excuse you. It doesn't matter. I overlook what you have done." That kind of forgiveness is not forgive-ness at all. At best, excusing says to the other person that he or she does not matter. At worst, excusing is a pretense and will not last.

Forgiveness says, "You have hurt me again. You have disappointed me again. You have taken me for granted or overlooked my feelings, or ignored me"—or whatever else we do to one another in a family. "You have become unjustly angry with me, you have let me down, you have misunderstood me, and yet … and yet— nevertheless—as God has forgiven me in Jesus Christ; as God has taken my sin to the cross and hidden it now in memoryless eternity, so I forgive you. I put the sin, fault, mistake away. I bury it in Christ. I cover it with the love of God in Jesus—and leave it in his memoryless hands."

That treasure allows us to wake up every day as if it were new. It allows us to blow through the house of our lives together and throw out all the clutter and junk that would keep us from one another. It allows us to love, to value one another, to respect the other (even when that other fails). It allows us to communicate—because we stand open and honestly before one another and forgive each other as God in Christ has forgiven us.

Easy? No. Never. Luther says that by the grace of God the old sinful self in us (and in our family) is daily drowned and dies, and a new self emerges full of the grace of God and able to do God's work and will.

The drowning part is not easy. It takes honesty and ability to admit our failures. It takes enough respect for the others in the family that we are able (really or figuratively) to get on our knees before them and ask for forgiveness. And it takes confidence to trust the grace of God where we find the power to forgive.

"You are the people of God. … You must forgive one another just as the Lord has forgiven you."

Questions/Activities for Reflection/Discussion

1. Finish this statement: "In our family, we communicate best when …" Reflect on (share) your response. What does your statement say about communication in your family? What is working well? What needs to be improved?

2. Describe the "house" of your family. What rooms are there? What activities go on in those "rooms"? What clutters the house of your family? What is getting in the way of your communication? What needs to be cleaned out? How can that cleaning be done?

3. Here are some phrases that might be said (should be said?) in a Christian home. Which are most important? Why?

- "I'm sorry"
- "Thank you"
- "I forgive …"
- "You are the best …"
- "I understand …"

Why are these phrases not usually heard often enough? What can you do in your family to make sure they are heard?

4. Take some time to think about (or share) one barrier to communication in your home—one that you can begin to deal with. What is that barrier? What makes it a barrier? What needs to be done to break it down? What does forgiveness have to do with that breaking? What steps might you take to begin breaking down the barrier?

5. **Family/Intergenerational:** Do a family sharing time. (Small groups can "become" a family for the time of this exercise.) Rules: Every person can speak. No criticism or blaming is permitted. Everyone has a right to say what is on his or her heart. Others will listen and reflect. No comments or defensiveness or trying to change the feelings of others is allowed. Sharing might start with phrases like these:

- "One thing that bothers me is …"
- "The best thing we do together is …"

- "I just dread …"
- "I look forward to …"
- "I am saddest when …"
- "I am happiest when … "

After the sharing time, talk about how some of the hurts can be done away with and the happy times increased. Make an appointment to meet again for a sharing time.

Option: Each person in the family writes a letter to the family telling his or her feelings right now. The letter should not blame, should not explain, should not complain. It should just say how that person is feeling. Get together at an appointed time so each person can read his or her letter to the family. The family accepts the letter as a gift—no comments, no corrections, no criticism. Each family member just listens. What did you learn? What did you learn that you can act on?

Spiritual Wellness

Characters

Pastor—*clerical attire*

Youth—*scruffy, dirty, like a street person*

Scene

The stage is near the chancel area of an empty church.

A pastor is in the church getting things ready for a coming service. The place is gloomy, like it is near night.

Youth comes in—wandering, looking around. He or she is near the pastor before the pastor notices youth.

Youth: Boy, this place is the weepiest—I mean Grimsville.

Pastor: Pardon?

Youth: This whole scene—it's too down—the pits. You mean people actually come here on their own, without anyone forcing them to?

Pastor: Yes, some do.

Youth: But why? Look at this! I mean, not a grin, not a smile. It's like a place for dead people. Crosses and hangings and … It's just too much.

Pastor: I take it this isn't the way you'd do the church?

Youth: Church? That's what you call it? People come here to do church—is that it?

Pastor: Yes, to worship together, to receive God's gifts and graces, to express …

Youth: Give me a break! Your words sound as phoney as these stained glass windows—so pretty but flat and lifeless. What does all that mean?

Pastor: It means that people come here because what we do here has meaning for them.

Youth *(passionate):* Meaning? This has meaning? Do you know where the people are coming from? Do you know what's out there? It's bad out there. It's the pits. Your fine people in their Sunday clothes, in their go-to-meeting smiles and pressed coats, have to live out there. It hurts to live out there.

Pastor: I know.

Youth *(scornfully):* Yeah, you know. What could you know about what's out there? You live in this unreal world full of stained glass windows and statues. What do they have to do with living, with hurting, with getting up in the morning, with the razor edge of another empty day?

Pastor: And what would you put here to make it fit those who live on the edge of pain and loneliness?

Youth: Well, you could at least wake the place up. People get enough gloom and doom. I mean, all you have to do is watch the evening news. People want to be happy, to be grinning out of their skins for a change. Now first thing, you ought to take that cross down. What does a cross mean? Put up a big smiley face. Tell them that God loves them and that everything is going to be all right. That's what people want to hear. Smile! Be happy!

Pastor: Is that what you want me to tell you? Smile, my friend. Don't worry! Be happy! Don't let life get you down. Just keep smiling, and everything will be all right. God doesn't really mind. God doesn't really care. Just keep a big grin on your face, your chin off the ground, your nose to the grindstone, your feet pointed straight ahead, your hands busy—and everything will be just peachy. Is that what you want to hear?

Youth: Nah, that's not for me. That's for the dopes. I'm different. I live on the edge. I've forgotten more pain than most of the fine-feathered people who sit in these benches ever even imagined. Listen, I grew up in the garbage can—thrown out with the junk. My mother died when I was three, and my father—I don't know what happened to him. I had to make it on my own. I learned to steal before I learned to talk. I learned to fight dirty, to be hard, to do it my way, to ignore the pain in my gut and the freezing nights. I learned to make it. You can't fool me with smiley faces. I can't be taken in by any God words and nice-sounding dreams of a cotton-candy world and a rose-colored future. Not me. I've been there. I know what's going down. Life is tough, hard …

Pastor: Like a cross?

Youth: Worse, like a torture rack—like a pain that won't let up—like an empty cell, like an empty room, like …

Pastor: Sweating drops of blood?

Youth: Yeah, and the worst part is that you have to face it all alone. I mean, no one cares. You can burn up or burn out or crack up, and no one cares a breath or a touch. It's almost like—like being …

Pastor: Abandoned by God?

Youth: Yeah, and all God does, if God is there, is look down with a tired eye at people who drag along like me and wonder if we're going to make it one more day. And if God is interested at all, he sends one more sharp edge to cut us, one more stone to break our back—and all the while he smiles. For God it's just a game—an I-don't-care game. What does God care for breathing dust like me? It's almost like …

Pastor: Carrying your own cross?

Youth: Yeah, now if God really cared … If God could really know what it's like to live a miserable screwed-up life like mine, to suffer the kind of pain that I suffer, to fail and fail, to be kicked around by people and by life … If God could know what it's like to be strung out and strung up and dying in the dust with no one near … If God could know, and really care …

Pastor: You might have time for him? And even for others who'd found him too? Is that right?

Youth: Yeah, kind of like that …

Pastor: My child, do I have a story for you …

Homily: Beyond Icing Religion

Reflection Text: May God himself, the God of peace, sanctify you through and through. May your whole spirit, soul and body be kept blameless [well, whole] at the coming of our Lord Jesus Christ. The one who calls you is faithful and he will do it. *1 Thess. 5:23–24*

Engaging the Listener

The mother came flying into the school room. She quickly backed the teacher into a corner and launched into her tirade. "You gave my Jimmy a D. How could you? And what does this note mean, "Needs special help with reading"? Jimmy is 10 years old. He's been in school for more than five years. If you people can't teach him to read in five years, what am I supposed to think? There's nothing wrong with my Jimmy except that he's had to spend his school years with incompetent, uncaring teachers ..."

In reality, Jimmy had a learning disability that was frustrating him to the point that he was giving up on his school work. In reality Jimmy needed help. But his mother chose to ignore the problem—to attempt to pretend that it was not there in the vain hope that somehow it would go away. It did not.

The young couple appeared to be the perfect match. They came from similar backgrounds and had similar interests and values. They seemed to enjoy each other's company. They seemed to spend most of their time together. "What a perfect couple," people would say. And the young couple would smile and nod and try to be the perfect couple they were supposed to be. Everyone was surprised when the marriage broke up. "How could that happen?" they all said. They seemed such a perfect couple.

In trying to be perfect, the young couple tried to ignore the hurts and the disappointments that were becoming increasingly clear to them. Because they were supposed to be perfect, they could not deal with their failings. In time, the failings became mountains—and destroyed their marriage.

Exploring Our Need

Everyone would agree that one of the secrets of a strong family is a "spiritual wellness"—a strength and depth of character, a cherishing of spiritual/eternal values, an open religious spirit. All of us have seen marriages and families that have that kind of strength. They are the ones we look to as examples of what our homes and families might be.

People who are in spiritually well relationships have the following characteristics:

- **Sense of purpose.** They are not drifting. They seem to be going somewhere.

- **Depth.** They do not simply live on the surface of the day—but they see and do at a deeper level.

- **Resiliency.** They don't break at the first problem. They don't fall apart when trouble comes. They seem to bend with the wind of difficulty and almost by nature come upright again.

- **Awareness of each other.** They are not a collection of individuals inhabiting the same space. They care about and care for each other.

- **Ability to look to the future.** They are not dwellers on the past nor terrified of the future. They move from today with confidence into their tomorrow.

- **Positive attitude toward life, toward each other.** They are able to laugh at themselves and their failings rather than dwell on the mistakes of the past. They see the world through—if not rose-colored—at least, realistically positive glasses.

And while we can describe a spiritually well marriage or family with phrases like the preceding—and we could add more—the truth is, that those that demonstrate these characteristics are rather rare.

If we could take time for confession, all of us would have to admit that our chances of becoming a "model" spiritually well family aren't very good—at least most days. In fact, we stumble often as we try to put in place the features of family living that will make our family strong and spiritually healthy. We mean to do better—to live and love in more depth; to stop looking at the past and bringing up faults; to stop being overbearing or blaming; to stop arguing and taking and demanding; to stop … The list could go on and on.

I wake in the morning. "Today, Lord, I will be different. Today I will be the "father knows best" you want me to be, Lord. Today I will be loving, forgiving, positive, encouraging—a perfect treasure to my family. I will hold my temper and repay even insults with joyful words of praise. Today, Lord, I will be what you want me to be"—that is, until I find my best toothbrush has become a tennis-shoe cleaner. Then … well, you know what happens then. For all of our good intentions, spiritual wellness eludes us.

Something similar happens in congregations. Though we know that congregations that are alive and well demonstrate a spirit that includes the same features as strong families—we have to admit that really spiritually well congregations are rather rare. As in families, congregations often demonstrate pettiness, bickering, me-firstism, blaming, a focus on the past, a tendency to ignore one another, backbiting, bitterness, anger, saving hurts from the past, a refusal to change—and on and on.

And it is not because God is not present. In the drama we saw, the young person was not spiritually well. He or she was lost, searching, unable to connect with others, confused, bitter—and yet, God was so evidently working in the life of that young person that the Gospel seemed to be made for him or her.

And most unfortunate of all, our solution to our failure to live up to our ideal of spiritual strength is to frost over our failings with a kind of nice-looking icing of pretense. We work to show to the world—and sometimes to each other—a sort of made-up goodness that we think will cover over the failings and make it all seem right somehow. We work to convince others (and we hope somehow that it will become true because we intend it to be) that we are the loving, caring, spiritually well group of people we are supposed to be. We are, after all, Christian people. We know, after all, how we are supposed to live. We work, after all, at being what God wants us to be.

We put on our Sunday manners and our loving face and try to convince everyone that as families we are models of spiritual strength and wellness and as congregations we are perfect pictures of what a group of committed Christians should be.

We substitute spiritual frosting for spiritual depth.

Applying the Good News

Every baker knows that there is a limit to the mistakes one can cover with frosting. Sooner or later, someone will cut the cake, pierce the frosting, and expose the disaster underneath. The same is true if our spiritual health in our families and in our congregation is a spiritual frosting.

In reality, we have to confess that we cannot make ourselves into the models of strength and spiritual wellness we want to be—that God wants us to be. It is exactly our struggling to be something we are not that lies at the heart of our failure.

We don't have the equipment to create love or

a positive attitude or acceptance or forgiveness or wisdom or commitment or strength. Whatever of these we manage to make for ourselves are, by definition, illusions—frosting that will, in time, be cut by testing or melt in the heat of conflict.

The source of all strength, wellness, depth—the perfecter of all relationships is God in Jesus Christ. And the first step in creating that wellness and strength is to admit to our God that we cannot do it ourselves.

"Lord, we've done our best, and it is not good enough. We've tried to make things right, but they often turn out wrong. With St. Paul, we have to say, 'What I want to do I do not do, but what I hate I do. … Who will rescue me from this body of death?' (Rom. 7:15). We come to you in repentance, seeking your forgiveness and the strength and health you offer in Jesus. Help and recreate us."

Repentance: the first step toward spiritual wellness. The step that must be constantly taken.

And then Paul's prayer for us brings wholeness: "May God himself, the God of peace, sanctify you through and through [make you entirely whole]. May your whole spirit, soul and body be kept blameless [well, whole] at the coming of our Lord Jesus Christ. The one who calls you is faithful and he will do it" (1 Thess. 5:23–24).

The perfection comes from God in Jesus Christ. We will be perfected. God is doing it. "Thanks be to God! He gives us the victory through our Lord Jesus Christ" (1 Cor. 15:57).

Questions/Activities for Reflection/Discussion

1. What was familiar about the young person in the drama? Which of his words touched you? Why? What of your own struggles did you hear? How does God's gospel of love in Christ touch those struggles?

2. Reflect on (share) a time when it seemed easier to try to ignore a problem or a painful situation rather than dealing with it openly. What was the outcome? Why does putting icing on something never work? What does honesty and openness have to do with our spiritual wellness?

3. Think of the spiritually strongest marriage or family you know. What are the characteristics that you admire? From where did those strengths come? What does endurance or perseverance have to do with the couple's or family's strength? How can you learn from them?

4. Why is "daily repentance and renewal" important for Christian living? How can that intentional repentance and forgiveness be a part of your home or family relationship? What strength might be the result?

5. **Family/Intergenerational:** Make a family "coat of arms." Draw a shape like a shield on a large piece of poster board or newsprint. (If your small group is made up of members of several families, make one for each family represented or one that you can all agree on.) This shield will tell all of the strength and character of your family. Divide the shield into sections. In each section, draw a symbol or write words that describe your family (or what your family would like to be like). These might include words like "our strength," "our hopes," "our history," etc. When the coat of arms is finished, share it with several other families, then post it at home and talk about what God's gifts have to do with making the coat of arms a reality.

Coping with Crisis

Scene

The stage area suggests a living room. Mother, Gail, and Tom sit on chairs, facing each other. The three sit for a time in silence. They are obviously very sad, looking down. Mother occasionally dabs at her eyes with her handkerchief.

Tom: When is Uncle Al coming to take us?

Gail: He said about twelve thirty. The funeral's not until two, you know.

Tom: I know. How can I think of anything else?

Gail: Mom, I'm worried about you. This is so hard for you. At the funeral home last night—and now this. How can you …

Mother: I'm all right, Gail. I'm wearing out these handkerchiefs, but that's what they're for.

Tom: It's strange. We knew this would happen some day. Dad's been fighting that bad heart for years. But not now …

Mother: You know, I think he knew it was coming. That last day, just before we went for the walk—oh, and he so loved to walk in the woods, down by the creek—called it "our creek." He said, "Mom, it's been a good life. The good times far outshine the bad. And best of all, we've done it together."

Gail: That sounds like him.

Tom *(with more passion):* What a crime! What a cruel joke! Millions of wretched people, evil people, people who don't even deserve to be alive are living and breathing and enjoying life—and he's *(pause)* gone …

Mother *(sobs):* I'll never get used to him not being here. How can I go on? How can I?

(Gail goes over to comfort her, hugging her so that her mother's head is on her shoulder.)

Gail: Oh, Mom, do you remember—way back when I was just a girl? I remember going with you to the hospital and waiting while you went to his room. That was the time

Characters

Mother—*about 60, dressed in black as for mourning*

Gail—*her daughter, about 40, also in mourning clothing*

Tom—*her son—in his late 30s, dark suit*

Al—*Mother's brother-in-law, also about 60, dark suit*

he had that heart attack—they didn't expect him to live. But he was a fighter. "They can't do me in yet," he said. And I remember riding on his wheel chair when they brought him out of the hospital. "Princess, this is my chariot, and I want you to ride in it with me," he said. All those years since then, Mom, all of them are a gift we should not even have had.

Mother: I know. I know God gave us more than we could even expect. But it's so hard to lose him.

Tom: I wonder what he'd say if he could talk to us now? I wonder what he'd have to say to the three of us. Probably something like he did at the supper table when we got too busy with complaining about our problems. "Lighten up," he would say. "The sun's in the sky and God's in his heaven and tomorrow will be better than today—if you want it to be."

Mother: But he couldn't always bring himself to believe that himself. I remember the time when the business almost went under—during the recession. I'd find him alone at night, sitting in the darkness with his head bowed. I never knew if he was crying or praying. But I'd start: "Dan, the sun's in the sky and God's in his heaven …" And then he'd look at me and smile and say, "And tomorrow will be a better day." And then we'd go back to bed.

Tom: So much life in him—even with his bad heart. Just last year, remember that fishing trip he and I took? Every time I think of it, I smile. He was so eager to go—even though he'd not been fishing for years. I showed him how to use the new spinning reel I got for him. He could never quite get it. *(He laughs.)* The lure kept flying straight up in the air or catching in a tree. But he stayed with it until he caught a bigger fish than mine—and he never let me forget it.

Gail: Daddy was so delightful sometimes. Remember the time he took me to the prom dance because the guy I was supposed to go with backed out at the last minute? When he said he was going to take me, I thought I'd die. How could I go to the dance with my father? And then when we walked into the gym, I must have turned eight shades of red. But before the evening was over, he was showing all the kids how to do the Charleston. *(She laughs.)* He was the life of the party—my Dad.

Mother: Maybe I never told you—oh, yes, of course, I did—about how we met. He actually fell for me the first time he saw me. I was walking on the street in our home town, and somehow—oh, you know the story.

Gail: No, tell it again, Mom. We want to hear.

Mother: Well, I was walking home from the store with these packages. And somehow one of them fell on the ground. And, of course, with the others, I couldn't see to pick it up. Your father was going by in his car. And all of a sudden he stopped right in the middle of the street, jumped out of the car, and ran over to pick up my package. He tipped his hat, just like they do in the movies, and then—and I remember this like it was yesterday—he walked right off the edge of the curb and fell flat on his face in the street. "Are you all right?" I called to him. "Sure thing," he called back from the gutter. "I always do a little fall, just so people will remember me."

(They all laugh together. Just as Al comes in.)

Al *(cross):* What is the matter? What's going on?

Mother: We were just remembering, Al. Just reminiscing.

Al: But laughing? It's the day of Dan's funeral. He's not even in the grave yet, and you're laughing. Don't you care that he's gone?

Tom *(angered):* Uncle Al, you have no right …

Mother *(interrupting Tom as she goes over to Al and puts her hands on his face):* Oh, Al. Don't you know we loved him like no one else in this world? He was so much a part of us that each of us will live with a piece of our heart missing from now on. We will shed tears on his birthday and on our birthdays and on Christmas and on every remembering of him. But when we remember, we'll also laugh—like he would have done. Think about it, Al. What would make Dan sadder than anything? What would ruin all that he did for us and gave to us?

Al: I don't know. I don't know what you mean.

Mother: If we would lose that spirit of joyful, expectant, hopeful living that he shared with us every day. If we became gloomy and morose and fell into empty self pity.

(She goes over to her children and puts her hand on their shoulders.)

Mother: No, Al. To laugh over his memory is no denial of how much that dear man meant to us. But to fail to laugh, to fail to hope, to fail to dream, to fail each other— that would be to deny him. God gave us a wonderful gift in that precious man. God made him the glue that holds us together as a family and gives us a reason to live for each other. And only when we can no longer laugh and hope and dream and trust in God for a better morning will we have forgotten him.

Homily: Tested Like We Are

Reflection Text: For we do not have a high priest who is unable to sympathize with our weaknesses, but we have one who has been tempted in every way, just as we are—yet was without sin. Let us then approach the throne of grace with confidence, so that we may receive mercy and find grace to help us in our time of need. *Heb. 4:15–16*

Engaging the Listener

H.G. Spafford lost all that he owned in the great Chicago fire. Shortly after that, his wife and children sailed to France on the *Ville du Havre,* one of the largest ships afloat. It was rammed by an English iron sailing vessel and sank to the bottom of the ocean within two hours, killing 226 people. Mrs. Spafford lived, but the four children were lost. As soon as it could be arranged, Mr. Spafford sailed to Europe to join his wife. On the way the captain indicated to him the spot where the tragedy had occurred. Spafford wrote the words to a hymn in the middle of the Atlantic over the exact spot where his four children had drowned a few days before. There in the dark of night, Spafford wrote these words: "When peace like a river attendeth my way, When sorrow like sea-billows roll. Whatever my lot, Thou has taught me to say, 'It is well, it is well with my soul!' "

Incredible strength. Which of us could do it? Researchers tell us that one of the characteristics of strong families is that they can cope with crisis.

Exploring Our Need

So my message for you is, If you want to have a strong family, go out there and do a better job of coping with the crises that come on you. Be tougher. Be stronger. Don't let life get you down. Don't bend or break under the troubles that come your way.

And, of course, that kind of help is an illusion. Telling ourselves or someone else to be stronger is kind of like telling ourselves or someone else to be taller. It might be a good intention, but in reality, not much changes.

Of course, we'd like it better if we were told that "strong families" don't have crises, or that they've learned some trick to avoid them. What we would really like is a lesson in preventing the crisis from coming at all.

Unfortunately, there are no easy ways to do this. A quick look at the lives of some of the great saints of God indicate that a faith relationship with Jesus may bring "peace" but it certainly does not bring ease.

Still some try to enlist God in their "getting away from trouble" game. Some try to make a talisman against trouble out of prayer or worship. Somehow, they believe, if they do enough to show God that they are sincere or trying or doing what is expected, if they ask enough or work at it enough, the trouble won't come. It's a strong belief. The converse, of course, is that when trouble does come, somehow God has let us down. "Why did God do this to me?" we hear. It is almost as if we are in a struggle with God to get God to do things our way, to give us what we think we deserve.

In truth we are in a struggle, but it is not a struggle with God. We are in a desperate struggle against "the wicked spiritual forces in the heavenly world, the rulers, authorities, and cosmic powers of this dark age" (Eph. 6:12 TEV), St. Paul tells us. Formidable enemies, to say the least. And this is no mock battle. It is a desperate struggle to the death. And though Jesus has already won the ultimate victory, and we are sure that "nothing [in all creation] can separate us from his love," yet we are certain to get wounded, bloodied, and eventually physically killed in the fight.

All of God's saints have been tested. Some beyond understanding. Read the history of the saints and martyrs. Many were killed in incredibly cruel ways. Others suffered the loss of everything. Though some popular preachers would like us to believe that we can work a bargain with God by which he will give us a pristine life and a big bank account, that is not true. The question is not, Will crises come? The question is, What will we do when crises come? When the crosses come, how will we carry them?

Applying the Gospel

The root of the word *crisis* is "crux"—the same base as cross. All families experience differences and difficulties. Sometimes conflicts. Sometimes problems. But these are transitory and often resolve themselves.

Crises are different. A crisis is an event that shakes the very foundation of our faith and our life together. It causes us to begin to question ourselves and others. It is an event of such proportion that it threatens to virtually destroy the family.

Some individuals, some families stand strong. Like Spafford. Like the family in the drama. Like others you have known. But these are not smarter people, more emotionally trained, somehow spiritually gifted people. These are not the unfeeling or the uncaring. They are those who know that the strength to stand in crisis is not something that comes from inside. There is no spiritual exercise one can do to build up our spiritual muscles so that we will be able to stand in times of crisis.

The strength comes from outside. From God. From the Savior. As a gift. Jesus was "tempted in every way, just as we are" (Heb. 4:15). Jesus walked the road of trouble, problem, conflict, and crisis for us and before us. Jesus walked the way to the ultimate crisis—the cross—and overcame. Part of the reason for the yearly recounting of that terrible journey of the Savior to the cross is to allow us to receive again the miracle of the Savior overcoming even our crosses.

"For we do not have a high priest who is unable to sympathize with our weaknesses, but we have one who has been tempted in every way, just as we are—yet was without sin. Let us then approach the throne of grace with confidence, so that we may receive mercy and find grace to help us in our time of need" (Heb. 4:15–16).

The promise of the Savior to be with us in the midst of all of the crises of life allows us to do the following:

- Face crisis positively—with hope. We know we can be crushed, but we will not be defeated. We can be hurt, but never overcome. We can even be killed, but not destroyed. We can confidently expect that out of every crisis that brings us down, God has a way of raising us new again.

- Face crisis together. We know that the pain of another can only be lessened as we share it. And we know that as we gather in Jesus' name, he is there with us. And we know that the very spirit of God is among us as we share. All crises lessen as we face them together.

- Expect resurrection. We have a confidence in the face of crisis that allows us to rejoice even in the midst of suffering. We know that even death brings resurrection.

A nonreligious friend attended my father's funeral. My father died suddenly and relatively young—in his mid-50s. After the service, my friend approached me. "I am sorry about the loss of your father, but I don't understand this funeral. It was like a celebration. What is there to celebrate in the loss of a loving and vital man like your father?"

What indeed? The same thing that we celebrate at any dead end we reach that brings us into a tomb of grief or self pity or despair. We celebrate the breaking of the tomb, the opening of new life, the destruction of despair. We celebrate resurrection.

How will you or I be able to face the next crisis that comes? We do not know. We know that we may be brought to our knees, thrown into a pit of pain, tested almost to the end of our endurance. But we also know that "in all things God works for good with those who love him … " (Rom. 8:28 TEV) and that the Spirit "comes to help us, weak as we are. … the spirit himself pleads with God for us in groans that words cannot express" (Rom. 8:26 TEV), so that we can be confident that nothing can "separate us from his love" (Rom. 8:38 TEV).

Only in the Savior and his promises do we stand ready to meet crisis.

Questions/Activities for Reflection/Discussion

1. Reflect on (share) a time of crisis in your life. What was the worst part of that crisis? How did it affect you? How did it affect your family? How did God reach out to you in that crisis? What resurrection did you discover?

2. A friend (family member) comes to you broken. "I am at the end of my rope," he or she says. "I don't know how to go on. I don't think I can find a way out. I think that God has abandoned me." How would you respond? What would you do? What would you say? How would you seek to be God's presence for that person?

3. "Why do bad things happen to good people?" Based on God's Word, how would you respond? Why do bad things happen to people who don't seem to deserve it? How does God's love in Christ shine through even those happenings?

4. Peter suffered through a crisis of his own making. Read Matt. 26:69–75. What was the nature of that crisis? How might Peter have described it? Read John 21:15–19. How was the crisis resolved? What does the outcome of Peter's crisis say to you about Jesus? about Jesus' love for you? about how we can expect our crises to come out?

5. **Family/Intergenerational:** Write a letter to your family (to yourself). Put in the letter the things you would like to hear the next time you are in a painful crisis. What would you want to say to yourself or to your family? Share the letter with others and members of your family. Save the letter and read it the next time you find yourself in a crisis.

Characters

Grandpa—*late 60s, casual clothing*

Josh—*grandson, about eight, play clothes*

Hank—*Josh's father, about 40, business suit*

Time Together

Scene

The stage area might suggest a backyard or basement.

Grandpa is working on an assembly of lumber with Josh, his grandson.

Grandpa *(lifting a board in place):* Where do you think we ought to put this one, Josh? About here look right?

Josh: Yeah, I think so, Grandpa. I think it needs that for the wings, kinda.

(Grandpa goes about nailing the board in place while Josh watches.)

Josh: Building an airplane is hard work, isn't it, Grandpa?

Grandpa: You bet. We've been working on this one for *(looks at his watch)* well, it must be at least a playtime and a half.

(Josh comes to sit by Grandpa, and they admire the craft.)

Josh: Grandpa, do you think it'll fly? I mean fly way up in the sky?

Grandpa: Why, Josh, there's no doubt about it. This plane will soar with the eagles.

Josh *(grinning):* Won't that be great, Grandpa? Up there in the sky zooming through the clouds?

(They both enjoy the image for a while.)

Josh: What's it like, Grandpa? I mean, up there flying in the sky?

Grandpa: Josh, my boy—there's nothing like it. When you're up in your plane, you'll be king of the world. You'll be soaring over everything stuck on the ground. There'll be no one to bother you or get in your way. It's just you and the sky and the wind. And down below you can see the people scurrying around like little ants. The tiny cars move along the silver ribbons of highways looking like penny toys under a Christmas tree.

Josh: And will she go far, Grandpa?

Grandpa: As far as the eye can see. Out over the mountains and up above the storms, you'll soar until the land runs out and you're out over the great ocean. If you want to, you can zoom down to watch the whales spouting their shower of breath over the rolling waves. Then you can fly down to Florida and give the big swamp a look. You can run a few alligators off the bank before you head out for the big gulf to see the dolphins playing in the sun on the shallow reefs. *(He pauses.)* Oh, Josh. There's nothing like flying.

(Again, they both sit and enjoy the reverie. Josh is partially leaning on Grandpa's shoulder.)

Josh: Grandpa?

Grandpa: What is it, Josh?

Josh: I think we need more lumber.

Grandpa: More? We've got quite a bit here, and there's some more over there.

Josh: But we got to make the plane bigger.

Grandpa: Bigger?

Josh: Yeah. It needs to be big enough for you and me. I don't want to go flying by myself.

Grandpa: Don't you worry, Josh, my man. I'll be there with you. That is, unless your daddy wants to go.

Josh *(after a pause):* I don't think he'll go, Grandpa. He's too busy for flying.

(Just then Hank enters. Josh tries to greet him, but Hank just tousles Josh's hair as he addresses his own father.)

Hank: Dad, for pete's sake. Where have you been? We were due at the lawyer's more than an hour ago. I told you we had to take care of those papers this morning.

Grandpa: I know. I reckon the papers will wait. I've got something more important to do here with Josh.

Hank *(astonished):* Josh? With Josh? *(To the boy.)* Josh, why don't you leave Grandpa alone now and go on and play? We've got some important business to take care of.

Grandpa: No! Wait! Hold it! I'm taking care of the important business—that is, Josh and me are. The lawyer can wait.

Hank: Dad, I just don't know what's wrong with you these days. You spend half your time playing with children.

Grandpa: I know. I missed a lot when you were Josh's age.

Hank: Well, that's enough play for now.

Grandpa: This is not play, my boy. This is work. Hard work—right, Josh? It's not easy to build a plane.

(Hank looks over the collection of wood somewhat scornfully.)

Hank: Aw, come on, Dad. That's not a plane. It's just some lumber. Why that wouldn't fly in a million …

Grandpa: Ah! Ah! Ah! Just take your time there. You still don't get it, do you, Hank? You still don't understand. *(Pause.)* Maybe it's my fault. Maybe I dumped reality and proper adult thinking on too many of your dreams when you were Josh's age. God knows, I'd give all the papers at the lawyer's office to do it over again.

Hank: But it's not a plane, Dad. Why kid the boy? It's just wood and nails. It won't fly. It can't fly.

Grandpa: Hank, my busy, successful, efficient son—how wrong you are. Why this plane has already flown half way round the world—up over the mountains and out over the ocean. Why just this morning Josh and I watched the whales turning in the waves. We dive-bombed the alligators in the everglades and caught the sparkle of the sun on the dolphins playing in the gulf stream.

Hank: Dad, that's just kid's stuff. That's just pretending. Is your mind going?

Grandpa: Going? No, Son, my mind is not going. I'm just spending time with my grandson, who still can fly imaginary planes that dance on sunbeams, who can fight the space raiders in the bedroom, and who can find a hidden treasure in the basement. I'm just spending time with my grandson before he grows and learns about lawyers and papers and money in the bank. Before his dreams turn to wanting and his pretending into grabbing what he thinks he needs. Now, still, while he laughs his way through the day run by a clock made by Mickey Mouse— I'm with him.

(Hank storms off.)

Josh: Grandpa, we don't have to finish the plane if you don't want to—if you have to go away with Daddy.

Grandpa: No. It's all right, Josh. This is a lot more important than the papers. The papers will be there long after you and I learn to attend to business and to properly shake hands the way grandfathers and grandsons are supposed to do.

Josh *(pondering):* Why is Daddy so mad all the time? Why doesn't he ever want to play?

Grandpa *(with a sigh):* I don't know, Josh. Maybe because I never taught him. When he was your age, I was the one who had to run to the lawyer and do the papers. I was the one who never had time. I left him with no one to build his planes or sleep in his tree house or fight the pirates down by the creek. I left him because I had to do what I thought was important. And now he's angry.

Josh: Grandpa, are you sad?

Grandpa: Yes, Josh. I'm sad for the boy I never had and for the boy he'll never know.

Josh: Well, you've got me, Gramps. *(He gives him a hug.)*

Grandpa: Oh, yes, Josh. I've got you. I've got you and this one more chance. Thank God for small boys, and airplanes that fly on two-by-four wings, and space invaders under the bed, and clocks that run on Mickey Mouse time. Thank God for you, Josh.

Homily: Giving Myself Away

Reflection Text: People were also bringing babies to Jesus to have him touch them. When the disciples saw this, they rebuked them. But Jesus called the children to him and said, "Let the little children come to me, and do not hinder them, for the kingdom of God belongs to such as these. I tell you the truth, anyone who will not receive the kingdom of God like a little child will never enter it. *Luke 18:15–17*

Engaging the Listener

The mother came to get her son from the principal's office where he had been sent for bad behavior. "Let me take him now," she insisted. "Why, what's the hurry? We need to talk," the principal protested. "I want to get him out of here before school is out," she said. "If the other children see him with you and tell their parents, what will they think of me?"

Then there's the old story about the mother who insisted that her children put on clean underwear before they go "into the city." "What if you are hit by a streetcar," she would say. "I don't want the undertaker thinking I'm a bad mother."

Indeed, there is a lot of pressure on parents. In our quick-to-blame-someone-else-for-what-we-do age, the buck often stops with the parents.

The dope dealer is not a bad person; he just comes from a bad environment. The young killer was abused, we say. The delinquent was unloved or unguided or undisciplined or "un"-something.

Exploring Our Need

And though parents are often unjustly blamed for what their children or their teens or even their grown children do, we know that what our children become does reflect on what we do for them and how we do it.

And we have it on good authority that children:

- above all need **consistency**, or they will grow up confused;
- above all need **acceptance**, or they will have a bad image of themselves;
- above all need **recognition**, or they won't have a healthy self-image;
- above all need **affirmation**, or they may not be able to form healthy relationships with others;
- above all need **responsibility**, or they may be immature all of their lives;
- above all need a **vision of the future**, or they may not have the confidence to be on their own;
- above all need **solid religious values**, or they may fall victim to all of the warped values that people want to sell them out there;
- above all need a **good example** to follow, or they won't know how to behave properly;
- above all need **respect**, or they won't respect themselves and others;
- above all need **to be loved**, or they will whither emotionally and never be able to love someone else fully;
- above all need to **feel safe**, or they will enter the world so fearful they may be paralysed and unable to function;
- above all need to feel **valuable**, or they will fail to value others;
- above all need **patience**, or they won't be patient with themselves;
- above all need **understanding**, or they will feel that they must deal with their troubles alone;

- above all need **to be heard**, or they will suppress their hurts and the emotional scars will distort their later life;

- above all need **spiritual and religious training**, or they will grow up lost and rootless;

- above all need a **sense of identity**, or they will grow up lost and wandering in the world;

- above all need …

Of course, the list goes on and on. We haven't even gotten to the basic needs like food and clothing; yet, the list is so long it would cover the whole front of our refrigerator. I want those parents who think they can manage all of that to stand up and receive an award.

Interestingly, what our children need is also what we need from each other. And indeed, not only our children, but our spouses need all of those things as well. Giving is the lifeblood of any relationship. Taking always brings deterioration and death. If we are not able to give love and respect and sympathy and patience and all of that to our spouse, our relationship will probably die.

And where is all of what we are supposed to give going to come from? Where are they going to find all of these treasures? From us, of course.

And what if they don't? Will we find them in our good intentions? in books? in strategies?

Then, when we have failed, again, we say: "Lord, it's too much. Really. How can I?"

Applying the Good News

It is interesting that we are told to receive Christ's kingdom as a child, that is, as a child aware that we are in need of love, care, affirmation, guidance, support, and understanding from God, too. The Bible is full of people in need of God. All the way back to the Garden of Eden, human beings were in need.

- Sometimes God sent judgment to call them back—to make them aware of their need for God.

- Sometimes God sent an agent—someone to rescue them. And there were many.

- Sometimes God sent a burning bush or a pillar of fire or a burning mountain.

- Sometimes God sent rules and laws to help people regularize their lives.

- Sometimes God sent a prophet to call people back.

- Sometimes God even sent catastrophes to make people aware of their need.

- God sent exile and trouble and promise and a good word.

But finally there was no substitute—no other way. God looked at you and me and said, "It's just not going to work. The rules and stories and laws and troubles and good times and bad times are not going to do it. I'll have to go myself."

That is what we celebrate this Lenten season—the coming of God in the flesh for us. The life and death of Jesus for us. The resurrection and promise of life for us.

We bring nothing to the relationship. It is fed and nourished by God's giving.

It's the lesson we need to learn as parents, as well. Certainly our children need all of those things from us. And they need even more—experiences and chances to learn and a rich environment. They need contact with interesting people and good education and a million other things.

But what will make them into what God is calling them to be is **us**—warts and failings and faults and problems and deficiencies and all. Us. The most precious gift we give is ourselves.

Self is the most precious gift God has given to us. Jesus gave himself, for us. No strings attached, no pay back, no performance standards, no status requirements. Jesus gave himself for us.

And, given power to do so by the gift of Christ, we do nothing less than give ourselves for our children.

Time only represents the giving of ourselves. The time we spend with our children, whether it is five minutes or five hours or five years—only has value as it represents our giving of ourselves. It is our expression of love. And, as the Bible says, "Love covers a multitude of sins."

We will never be perfect parents or spouses. We will never know all the answers or get every response right. We will never even understand all the questions. But we have been given a gift that makes it possible for us to give our children what they really need: we give ourselves. We offer ourselves to each other—unwrapped, unpolished, less than perfect. We offer ourselves with the knowledge that God in Christ will make us right before him and right for each other.

To the world, it makes no sense to give yourself away. To the takers of the world, to do so is foolish, naive, silly. To those who measure success by gain and get into relationships for what they can get out of them, giving self makes no more sense than did Jesus' walk to the cross.

But we know that we are all children before God. We all come to Jesus for a blessing. We all cluster around to receive the gift of himself. And we all receive his power to be the children of the world who do nothing less than give ourselves away.

Questions/Activities for Reflection/Discussion

1. Think back to your childhood. Reflect on (share) your relationship with one other person who gave you quality time—gave of self to you. What motivated that person? What memories do you cherish? What place does that person have in your personal "hall of fame"? What does the example of that person say to you?

2. Someone has said, "Time is the most valuable commodity in the world." Do you agree or disagree? Why? When do you feel you use time well? When do you feel you waste it? Why?

3. Look up and read or reflect on several Bible stories about children: "David, Chosen and Anointed," "The Boy Samuel," "Jesus in the Temple," "Jesus and the Children." What do these stories tell you about children? about God's attitude toward children? What can we do as a family and as a congregation to value, help, include, and enhance the spiritual lives of our children?

4. A common lament of parents of older children is, "I should have spent more time with them." Why is that feeling so common? What failing does it see? What is the value of the feeling? In a sense, it is "never too late." Why? What does God have to do with making sure that we don't feel that kind of failure?

5. **Family/Intergenerational:** Write out a plan (personal or family) for a coming week. In each section of the day, write the activity you likely will be doing (e.g., school, work, shop, TV). Beside each activity, write the name of the person most benefited by that activity. Go over your week. How many activities are for self? How many are for others or for other people or families? What does the chart say about how you might change your plans? How can remembering God's gift of love in Jesus help us with our activity planning?

Cross Points

Six Dramas

Introduction

Life is full of crises: cross points at which we must choose to move in new directions. Many "self-help" books claim to be able to empower us to move through crises and choose the "healthy" way. In reality, crises often paralyze us. They expose our frailty and bring us quickly to the end of our ability to cope. At that point, at that cross point, the Gospel of Jesus Christ touches us, comforts and empowers us to move from "death to new life." The six dramas (two monologs, two dialogs, two short plays) in this series can form the core of a series of six worship experiences that look at the crises of life in the light of the cross of Jesus Christ. Each drama is accompanied by a homily and set of discussion/reflection questions for use in worship or other congregational settings. The titles and themes for the dramas are as follows:

Crisis—Guilt/Forgiveness

Theme: How Can I Know I Am Forgiven?

Gospel Focus: God made him [Jesus] who had no sin to be sin for us, so that in him we might become the righteousness of God. *2 Cor. 5:21*

Drama: *What Have I Done?*

†

Take Up the Cross—Discipleship

Theme: Can I Bear Jesus' Cross?

Gospel Focus: If anyone would come after me, he must deny himself and take up his cross and follow me. *Matt. 16:24*

For my yoke is easy and my burden is light. *Matt. 11:30*

Drama (Monolog): *The Woman at the Well*

†

Cross Point—Choice Point

Theme: How Can I Choose?

Gospel Focus: I can do everything through him who gives me strength. *Phil. 4:13*

Drama: *Waiting for Me*

†

Cross Bearing—Burden for Another

Theme: Bear One Another's Burdens

Gospel Focus: Whatever you did for one of the least of these brothers of mine, you did it for me. *Matt. 25:40*

Drama (Dialog): *The Voice*

†

The Cross of Suffering

Theme: God, Why me?

Gospel Focus: My power is made perfect in weakness. *2 Cor. 12:9*

Drama (Monolog): *The Monster*

†

The Final Cross

Theme: Will I (Will God) See My Life As Ended or Completed?

Gospel Focus: For to me, to live is Christ and to die is gain. *Phil. 1:21*

Drama (Dialog): *Peter's Last Visitor*

†

Using These Dramas

These dramas are intended for use in worship. They could be part of a series of six worship experiences (e.g., for Lent). The dramas have these features in common:

- They require few "actors" and little rehearsal. The parts can be read, if time to memorize is not available.
- They require little scenery (only enough to "set the stage") and minimal costuming.
- Most of the parts can be adapted to men or women. Young people (with a little makeup when they need to look older) enjoy doing dramas like these.

- They can all be done in a worship setting. Since they require minimal "space," performing the dramas in a chancel area would work well.

They can also be performed at a congregational "family night" or in other gatherings. Whether used in worship or another setting, the dramas are intended to "open the subject" and help people think about and begin to relate the crisis issue featured to their own lives. The dramas can be followed by one of the following:

- A time of silent reflection.

- A time of small group discussion (questions for discussion are included).

- A time of family interaction (an intergenerational activity is suggested for each drama). In a congregational setting, these intergenerational activities can be done by small groups (groups of five or six that include people of varying ages).

- The homily included in this resource or another.

- An open discussion time that includes a panel presentation or debate.

These resources also could form the core of activities at a "spiritual enrichment" retreat done in the church building or away. Each of the dramas, followed by the homily and a time of discussion and interaction, could form six "learning sessions" at an overnight retreat or an all-day enrichment workshop. A retreat-type setting would provide ample time for groups to do the intergenerational activity suggested with each drama.

About Staging

Each of these dramas suggests a specific setting. Some of the settings are important to the drama itself. But none of the settings are elaborate. In a worship area, the setting for the drama can be simply suggested with a few props. A couch indicates a living room. A table suggests a kitchen. Since the dramas all turn on the relationship of the characters, the setting is only background. Audiences will quickly focus on the characters. At that point, the setting becomes irrelevant. For that reason, you will want to keep your staging and the props you use as simple as possible.

A drama in two scenes

Characters

Barry—*a young, single professional*

Jane and **Herm**—*young couple, about Barry's age*

Kay—*elderly woman, in wheelchair*

What Have I Done?

Scene 1

Stage area suggests a messy room with at least three chairs. Barry is dressed in casual clothes that look like he slept in them. He slouches in a chair. He sits, staring ahead of him; television is off.

The doorbell rings. Barry responds without much enthusiasm. He returns leading Herm and Jane, dressed for an evening out. During the first few exchanges the three are seated facing each other.

Herm *(brightly):* Barry, my boy. It's good to see you again. We've missed you around church and all.

Barry *(flat voice):* I know. I know. It's good to see you both too. Been really busy, you know. Lots of deals in the fire. *(He laughs uncomfortably.)*

Jane: We thought for sure you'd be at the Christmas party last week—you know, the one at the Dobson's? But, no Barry. And I said to Herm right then, I said, "We've got to go check on old Barry. Maybe he's ill or something."

Barry: No. No. Nothing like that. *(He pauses and speaks in a somewhat distant voice.)* Just busy.

Herm: And there's the men's retreat in a couple of weeks, and I noticed that you weren't signed up. You always go along on that one, Barry.

Barry: Always? Not always. I've been to a few. But this time, I … Well, I'm … I'm not sleeping too well. I think I'd better take a rain check.

Jane *(kidding):* New woman in your life, Barry? Come on. You can tell us. You can't keep secrets from good friends like us.

Barry: No. As a matter of fact, I haven't been dating much lately. I've been kind of trying to keep on top of things at work …

Jane *(looking around the room):* And around home too, I presume.

Barry *(laughs weakly):* I never was much good at cleaning up. You know that. Stuff like that kind of gets away from me.

Herm *(standing, hesitating):* Well, we might as well come out with it, Barry. We're worried about you, guy. This is just not like you, holed up here in your room, not getting out with people. What's the matter? Anything we can do?

Barry: Nothing. Nothing's the matter. I'm just working … working on …

Jane: Listen, Barry. I hate to bring this up, but you just have not been the same since the accident.

Barry: Oh, the accident. *(Long pause.)* I don't think about that much anymore. Really. It was just an accident.

Herm: Your neighbor, wasn't it? Terrible thing. How could that have happened?

Barry *(shaking his head, as if trying to clear it):* I really don't want to talk about it.

Jane *(plunges on):* I heard that she stepped right in front of your car. Mrs. Wilson, wasn't it?

Barry: Yeah, Kay Wilson from down the block. Funny, she never went out that time of day. I never saw her out that early in the morning. But there she was all of a sudden. Stepped right out from behind the cars—so quick. She could move so quickly for an … *(Pause.)* What could I do? I didn't see her. I didn't see …

Herm: And you were cleared of all the charges, weren't you, Barry? I mean, they didn't think you were responsible.

Barry: No. No charges. I was cleared. *(He becomes animated.)* It wasn't my fault. I was just driving along. She stepped out in front of me. *(He is adamant.)* It wasn't my fault.

Jane: And how is she? I mean the woman? How is she now?

Barry: I … I think she's okay. They moved her to a home. She couldn't take care of herself at her apartment anymore after … after … I mean, she needed some help, so they took her to a home somewhere.

Herm: You don't know where?

Barry *(very defensive):* Why should I? She's nothing to me. I hardly knew the woman. Her son takes care of her—or someone. She doesn't need me. I sent her flowers in the hospital. I sent her a card. My insurance company even paid for part of her treatment—even though they didn't have to. *(Angry.)* What else am I supposed to do? It wasn't my fault. Don't you understand? It wasn't my fault.

Herm *(surprised at his intensity):* Take it easy, guy. We weren't accusing you of anything. Just wondering.

Barry: Well, you can wonder somewhere else. *(He starts to rise.)* I'm busy now, if you don't mind …

Jane: But Barry, we want to see you back with us, with the gang. We don't want you to just waste away …

Barry *(still angry):* I'm not wasting away. I'm happy. See, I'm smiling. My life is great. Work is good. Things are going fine. I don't need people like you to take care of me.

Herm: Don't you?

Jane: Barry, we just wanted you to know that we care—care about you. I think you're carrying a lot of pain from that accident. I think you should go and see Kay Wilson and talk to her and …

Barry *(sarcasticly):* And apologize? Ask for forgiveness, I suppose? *(Emphatically.)* Well, I'm not guilty. I didn't do anything. I'm not responsible. Don't you understand? Don't you believe that?

Jane: A better question might be, do you believe it?

(Darkness or a pause indicates the passage of time.)

Scene 2

Stage area suggests a room in a nursing home. Kay, an elderly woman, sits in a wheelchair. There might be a hospital-type bed in the background. She is reading, holding a book in her lap.

Very quietly, Barry enters. He's got a bunch of flowers. He stands in the background looking at her for a long time. Finally she looks up at him.

Kay: Oh. I didn't realize someone was there. Come over so I can see who it is. I do love company. Come nearer, here in the light.

Barry *(fumbling):* Oh, no. It's all right. I just stopped by to … It's not important. I think I'd better be going.

(He turns to leave and hesitates.)

Kay: Barry. It's you, isn't it, Barry?

Barry: How did you know? How …

Kay: I know you, Barry. We were friends over on Maple, don't you remember? We would always walk to the grocery store together on Saturday mornings. We did that so often. Don't you remember?

(He begins to move slowly over toward her.)

Barry: Sure, I remember. You were always a little quicker than I was. *(She laughs a little.)* You were pretty fast on your feet for …

Kay: For an old dame? Isn't that what you used to say, Barry? For an old dame?

Barry *(embarrassed):* I didn't mean anything by it.

Kay: Oh, I know, Barry. I used to look forward to our Saturday meetings. You would always make me laugh. Do you remember how we would laugh?

Barry *(fumbling for something to say):* I brought you these flowers. I thought they might make you feel … *(He drops them on the table or bed.)* I guess they don't mean much.

Kay: But it does mean something that you came, Barry. I've wanted to talk to you since … since the accident.

Barry: I know. I'm really sorry about that. But I was awfully busy with … with all the … with work and all and I couldn't … *(He pauses.)* It wasn't my fault, you know. It wasn't my fault that I hit …

Kay: Oh, I know, Barry. It was my own foolishness. I was in a hurry. I should never have walked out that way.

(He is standing beside her and suddenly drops to his knees, putting his arms around her.)

Barry: Oh, my God, Kay. What have I done? What have I done to you?

(He drops his head to her lap, and she pats his head, like one might comfort a child as he weeps in her lap.)

Kay: It's all right, Barry. It wasn't your fault.

Barry: Kay! Can you ever forgive me? Can you forgive me?

Kay: Forgive you? Forgive you? Why, Barry, don't you know that you are already forgiven.

Barry *(raising his head to speak):* Oh, God. If I could only believe that. Look what I've done. Look at you. Look what I've done.

Kay: Barry, that's why I wanted to talk to you. I was afraid you'd take this on yourself. I wanted you to know that I have already forgiven you. And God has forgiven you.

Barry: Has he? Has God forgiven me?

Kay: You know he has. God forgives drivers who don't look and foolish old women who walk out between parked cars and friends who forget to show their love and even foolish children who can't seem to forgive themselves.

Barry: Oh, God! Forgive me!

(With great gentleness, she reaches out and wipes the tears from his eyes.)

Kay: Barry, my friend. I have forgiven you, and God has forgiven you. Now you have to forgive yourself.

(She holds his head on her shoulder for a while. Then he rises, wiping the tears from his eyes.)

Barry: Can I come and see you again?

Kay: You'd better. I'm still looking forward to our next trip to the grocery store. I'll bet you I can still beat you.

Barry *(with tenderness):* I know. You're pretty fast for an old dame.

(He holds her hand for several beats, then bends over and kisses her on the cheek.)

Barry: Thank you, my friend.

(Barry lets her hand slip from his and exits.)

Homily: Crisis— Guilt/forgiveness

Theme: How Can I Know I Am Forgiven? Gospel Focus: God made him [Jesus] who had no sin to be sin for us, so that in him we might become the righteousness of God. *2 Cor. 5:21*

Engaging the Listener

He came for counseling. An affable man, he was a success by any standard. He carried a sense of confidence about him. He wore only the best suits. He had, after all, established a successful business of his own. His family was exemplary. He was a pillar of the community.

And yet … and yet, he feared he was becoming an alcoholic. And there seemed to be no cause—except for the pain he felt inside himself. A pain he kept hidden. A pain he could not make go away.

He could not say the words—he did not even know them yet—but in time he would say with the psalmist: "Have mercy on me, O God, according to your unfailing love … cleanse me from my sin" (Ps. 51:2).

In the drama, Barry said: "Can you ever forgive me? Can God ever forgive me?"

Exploring Our Need

In the drama, Barry looked for some way out of his guilt. Not me. I am not responsible. I'm not the one … Am I? And he could not escape the light of his own memory.

Though it may be possible to keep the lights of our own awareness fixed firmly on the "right now" of living, sometimes something happens (like Lent, perhaps) to drive us into life's basement.

Ready or not, as unappealing as it may sound: it's time to clean the basement. Not the basement at our house, the basement of our lives.

Think of your life like a house. Most of the time we live on the first floor of our lives—not in the basement where the hidden things are. We live on the first floor, the brightly lit floor, the now floor. The place where things happen.

Our house has a living room for family activities; it has a work room—where we are employed; it has a recreation room, probably filled with toys; it has a kitchen for meals and interaction; it probably even has a small room at the back for "religious" activities.

The first floor of our lives is the place where relationships happen, where activities go on. It's the place where we control what face we want people to see. It's the place of doing, not thinking; of acting, not planning; of busyness, not reflection. Here, on the first floor, relating to people happens in quick exchanges: there is a lot of empty talk about weather and how we are or are not feeling. There is a lot of storytelling designed to cover what is really going on. And there is a lot of overlooking—of quick excusing, of saying, "pardon me" and "I'm sorry."

Upstairs is more private. There we keep our future. Some of it is dark—we cannot know what it will be. But up there also we keep our wants and hopes and dreams. We occasionally take someone up there with us—but only a select few.

Most of the time we get along on the first floor (with a few quick trips upstairs) pretty well. We live on the first floor day to day, making our way.

Of course, we know the basement is there. Down there is the darkness of remembering, the hidden faults and guilts, and the broken promises—all of it carefully stored on shelves. Down there we find the face in the mirror we don't want to see; there is the self we don't want to show. There are the things we can't put away. Unfortunately, the basement does not always stay safely closed.

The man who came for counseling had to clean up the basement. The pain of what was there would not let him have any peace. Barry had to clean the basement—he could not face the reality of what he had done.

Sometimes we are driven into the basement by events: a mistake we can't make right; the destruction of a relationship; the failing of our good intentions. Quickly we come to the end of our ability to pretend that all is well. Quickly we confront the questions that probe and accuse: Is it my fault? What have I done? What have I failed to do? How can I face this? How can I go on?

There we stand, amid the ashes of our past and the rubble of what we meant our life to be and say, "God, look at this mess. How did this happen? I cannot clean it up. I don't know where to start. I cannot remake the mirror image of myself. I cannot undo what is done. Look—but don't look at this rubble, this garbage of my self and soul. 'God, be merciful to me …'"

Applying the Good News

That's what Lent is about. It is not (as some have said) a time for wallowing in negatives. It is not a tired remnant from the past. It is, very simply, a time to open the basement. It is a time to do that single, healing, helpful thing that will make all the difference: It is time repent.

How desperate, how futile the visit to the basement would be if all we could do there was to try to cover the rubble of the past with more darkness. How terrible if all we could do was to run in terror from the pain of the past, slam the door to the basement again, and hope we never have to go down there again.

But that is not the outcome. "God made him [Jesus] who had no sin to be sin for us, so that in him we might come the righteousness of God" (2 Cor. 5:21).

The message is deceptively simple, incredibly transforming: "Barry, don't you know that you are already forgiven?"

My child. God's child. You with the darkest of basements and the most painful collection of should-have-beens and should-not-have-beens. My child. God's child. Don't you know that in Jesus Christ you are already forgiven?

Look. Look carefully now. The basement is full of light. The basement of your life is cleaned once again. The rubble is thrown out forever. The pain is gone.

Lord, here we come again. Again to the altar of your forgiveness. We come covered with the ashes of what we have made of ourselves, our lives, our dreams, our good intentions. "Lord, be merciful to us …"

And God says again, "My child. Don't you know you are already forgiven?"

Questions/Activities for Reflection/Discussion

1. Take an imaginary trip to the basement of your life. Reflect on (share) one thing you find there that troubles you. Where did that come from? What does guilt have to do with your feeling? How can the light of Christ's forgiveness help you get rid of what troubles you?

2. "Christian families (congregations) are not perfect, just forgiven." What difference does that truth make? How does the truth of God's constant forgiveness make a difference in the way we deal with each other?

3. A friend comes to you. "I've done something that God cannot forgive," he or she says. "It is too terrible. God cannot care for me anymore. God seems so far away. I don't think I can reach God." What would you say? How would you help?

4. Read Col. 3:8–17. How does Paul describe our "new life" together in Christ? How

does that description fit your family? your congregation? What does forgiveness have to do with that new life? How do we get the strength to live the "new life"?

5. **Family/Intergenerational:** Make two posters (use poster board or cardboard) for your family (or for each family in your small group). Write the words "I am sorry for ..." at the top of one. Write "I forgive you for ... " at the top of the other. Leave lots of blank space, but decorate the posters with reminders of God's forgiveness: symbols, words of promise, etc. In your home, use the posters to remind yourself to ask for forgiveness and to give it. Family members can write their mistakes on the first poster or words of forgiveness on the second. Talk about how it feels to be forgiving and forgiven.

A monolog in one scene

Character

Woman—*middle-aged, simple, Bible-times clothing*

The Woman at the Well

Scene

Stage area might suggest a location near a Bible-times well where water is drawn. The monolog can be done, however, with no stage props.

Woman enters and moves near to what appears to be a well. She is carrying a water pot with a handle and a ladle in it. She speaks directly to the audience after standing quietly, reflecting for several moments.

Woman: This is where I first met him … the one they call the Rabbi … that one who talked to me … the one who knew me … who said he was going to give me living water. *(Pause.)*

(She laughs.) Water. I wish he'd only given me water. Water I could handle. Water would help me. He gave me something all right—something more than water. *(Pause.)*

You know, I thought I had trouble before I met him. I used to complain about the problems I had to deal with every day. But they're nothing compared to what's happened to me since.

(She struggles to explain.) It's like he turned my life upside down, like everything that used to make sense doesn't anymore, like my heart—my mind—my will were all taken from me and turned inside out and put back into me … and I don't even seem to recognize them … recognize myself anymore.

I know that sounds crazy. How could all that happen by just meeting someone … talking to someone? How could it happen? *(Pause.)* And to tell you the truth, I don't even know the answer.

Oh, I've "talked to" a lot of men in my day. Certainly more than those proper ladies who live up on the hill think I should have. The men I knew were all such nice talkers. They told me what I wanted to hear. They gave me words that they thought would reach me. But they were takers too. They were out to use me, to take advantage, to get what they could. I've been around. I know how all of that works.

And yet …

And yet he was different. He didn't want anything from me. He didn't look at me—he looked through me. He didn't just see me with his eyes—he saw me with his heart. He didn't just talk to me—he talked into me, into my spirit, into my soul. And I've not been the same since. *(Pause.)*

Maybe I should have gone with him—at least that might have been easier—easier than staying and living with … with the hurt. *(Pause.)*

Oh, it seemed all right at first. It all seemed so easy when he first talked to me. It was like he knew me better than I knew myself. And suddenly there was … I don't know … a kind of peace I'd never known before.

(She reflects.) You know, life's been hard for me. I've been down a lot. I don't even remember my parents, and the man who first sold me when I was 15 had already raped me. And then there were the other men like that big, brave soldier who was going to be my husband and give me all the things I wanted. Oh, he could promise—promise all the things he'd bring back from this place or that and the gifts he was going to buy me. *(She pauses. There is longing in her voice, remembering with some sadness.)* Then, that last time, he just never came back. I don't even know what happened to him. Maybe he died … *(Pause.)*

I don't know. I guess I got used to the life I had. It wasn't much, but I could make it from day to day through the men who thought they had a claim on me, through the asking and the taking and the scorn of the people of the town.

(She laughs.) Most of the townsfolk wouldn't even look at me. And some of the women—those fine, proper women from across town—would even spit at me. Like I was an animal, they would spit at me.

(Bolder.) But I didn't need them. I had my own life to live. I knew where I was going, what I was doing. *(She grows quieter.)* And most of the time I didn't even notice that empty place down inside—that place that ached at night when I couldn't remember what bed I was in, that

dark place that would be there each morning with questions I could not answer.

Until …

Until he came. The Rabbi. The Master. The Messiah, he said. He asked for nothing and claimed everything. He demanded nothing and gave everything. He spoke hardly a hundred words to me, and yet he changed my life.

Oh, Lord … how you changed my life!

(Now with pain.) But they don't believe me, you know. Even now with what he gave me—even with all of that—I hurt so bad sometimes.

My friends. *(She laughs.)* Oh, yes. My friends. They won't have anything to do with me anymore. I might as well have gotten leprosy. They think I'm crazy. Really. They think I'm right out of my mind to believe—to trust—that Jew … that man … *(pauses, more reflective)* that wonderful, mysterious man.

And, of course, the good people in town still don't have any room for me. They don't believe I could have changed from what I was before. They can't seem to see into my heart like he did. They don't hear the new words in my mouth or understand my thoughts and my hopes and my dreams—all so different now. So different … *(Pause.)*

I should have gone with him. At least, he would have had time for me. He would have listened to me, understood …

There's no one now. No one. And not even this water quenches my thirst.

(She speaks more quickly.) I thought about going back—back to the way I was before. It would be so easy to do. I know that life so well. I know how to survive among the takers and the robbers and the users. I know how to be hard enough, strong enough, mean enough to get by. It would be so easy, and so secure, and so …

But I can't. *(Stronger.)* I can't do it. The pain of this thirst is nothing like that great, gaping hole of nothingness that used to be inside me—that great circle of darkness that would make even my laughter sound as hollow as a tomb.

I can't go back. I can't turn away from being at home with myself, with my God … I can't go back to that deadly pain that racked my spirit and brought me down into death—even while I was still breathing. I can't go back to the fear and the struggle—where there was no peace, no hope …

Now, still … here … here alone with no one to hear me … alone with no one to hold me or care for me or even try to understand me … here where he reached me and gave me life … here I know I'm alive and that the life that he gave me is a gift from God to be cherished. I know that because of him I am held by God, and God will not let me go—will never let me go whether I am in the pits of despair or alone in an endless wilderness or even on the heights of my own imagining. God will not leave me.

He promised. I saw the promise in the eyes of that one who cared enough to give me living water. Because he promised, I drink this water … this gift … this life. *(She drinks from the ladle.)*

(She offers the ladle to the audience.) And I offer it to you. Come. Here. Take this water from me—this water of life. It was a gift to me. Come. Take it. It will change you. It will make you into someone you might not even know. Take it. It will turn your life inside out. It will change your heart. It will open your eyes …

And in spite of the tears you may find after you drink, in spite of the hurt that might fill you as you try to follow, in spite of the many who will never understand you, who will ridicule you and turn away from you, in spite of it all, you will be alive and whole and at peace, perhaps for the first time in your life.

Come and drink with me.

This water will become in you a spring of water gushing up to eternal life.

To life—with him.

Homily: Take Up the Cross—Discipleship

Theme: Can I Bear Jesus' Cross?
Gospel Focus: If anyone would come after me, he must deny himself and take up his cross and follow me. *Matt. 16:24*
For my yoke is easy and my burden is light. *Matt. 11:30*

Engaging the Listener

The people of the town had become very wealthy. Everything seemed to go their way. Their crops sold well. Their businesses prospered. Everything in the town did well, that is, except the church. As wealth increased, the number of those gathered on Sunday morning dwindled. Finally, out of money and out of members, the church closed. "This relic will never open again," the mayor said. The town leaders agreed.

The closed building fell into disrepair. Then one Sunday, some of the people on the way to their parties and picnics noticed a lone young girl kneeling on the steps of the church in front of the locked doors. When they returned some time later, she was still there. In fact, they began to notice that every Sunday morning she would be there alone, kneeling on the hard wooden steps, apparently praying.

Some got rather aggravated. "What right does she have to make a spectacle of herself like that?" they carped. "She'll catch her death of cold," one said. Others, trying not to look at her, agreed that she'd soon tire of the whole thing.

Tire she did not. In fact, after several months, one or two others began to join the young girl. Now the townspeople noticed, not just the lone girl on the steps, but an elderly woman, and the young man who worked at the hardware store, and a mother with two of her children.

Every Sunday they gathered. Every Sunday they simply knelt and prayed. Every Sunday, it seemed, someone else joined them. Winter arrived, and still the group continued with their Sunday gathering.

Finally, in desperation, the leaders of the town had a meeting. This could not go on. Someone could get sick or hurt or worse. How would that look for the town?

"There's nothing to do but open the church," said the mayor. And they all agreed.

"How could this happen?" someone asked. "How could that dead church be opened again by a single young girl?"

"How indeed?" said another.

Exploring Our Need

Disciple (Greek—Mathētēs): One who has been taught or instructed. One who follows the teacher.

Jesus' disciples were easily identified. They followed him. Find Jesus; find his disciples. They did not hide. Their faces were familiar. Even their accent betrayed them (Matt. 26:73).

Not so today. It's hard sometimes to tell who is a disciple. As Jesus' followers, we don't talk or dress differently, except perhaps for an occasional piece of jewelry. Very likely, one could watch us a long time and never even know we are followers of Jesus.

Think about this: Suppose we did mark ourselves. Suppose as modern disciples we wore an "I am a follower of Jesus" uniform of some sort. Perhaps at Baptism we might all put on a white outfit with an emblazoned cross on the front.

The idea has possibilities. We would be easily identified and able to identify one another. We might even recognize more accomplished disciples by adorning their uniforms with bars or ribbons for years of faithful service. (Remember the Sunday school attendance awards?)

Of course, uniforms have their drawbacks too. How would we deal with the attention (hatred? scorn?) we would get from the people of the world? Perhaps it would be easier to put our uniforms in the back of the closet and only get them out on Sunday. After all, we would not want to make a spectacle of ourselves by wearing them on the street or to work or to the places we go for entertainment.

That is, we might be tempted to hide our uniforms—until the going got tough and we needed to hear good words from Jesus. In times of trouble, uniforms firmly in place, we would seek to savor again the gentleness of his call and the wonderful promises that attend his beckoning:

- "Come to me, all you who are weary and burdened, and I will give you rest. Take my yoke upon you and learn from me, for I am gentle and humble in heart, and you will find rest for your souls. For my yoke is easy and my burden is light" (Matt. 11:28–30).

- "If you hold to my teaching, you are truly my disciples. Then you will know the truth, and the truth will set you free" (John 8:31–32).

- "I have come that they may have life, and have it to the full" (John 10:10).

- "My sheep listen to my voice; I know them, and they follow me. I give them eternal life, and they shall never perish; no one can snatch them out of my hand" (John 10:27–28).

- "Peace I leave with you; my peace I give to you. … Do not let your hearts be troubled and do not be afraid" (John 14:27).

How often we need to hear those words. Yes, Lord—in the middle of this muddled world full of false promises and fading hope; in this frightening, violent, darkened world; in the midst of the hurts and confusion that often plague us—we are following. What else can we do? Where can we go but to the one who loves us with an eternal love?

So, in response, we put on the uniform. At least to the best of our ability we seek to live as Jesus' disciples. We go to church more or less regularly (many people, even church members do not). We try to discipline our children, if not our tongue. We pray before meals—sometimes even in public places. We see that our children are baptized and haul them to confirmation classes. We might even serve on a congregational board, teach a class, sing in the choir—things like that.

Perhaps if God gave disciples awards for good discipleship, sometimes at least we'd have a cluster of modest ribbons on our uniform that would show our dedication, our commitment, our active discipleship …

But before we take too many bows, let's look again at how Jesus describes the life and actions of his disciples:

"Whoever acknowledges me before men [like wearing a uniform perhaps?], I will also acknowledge him before my Father in heaven. But whoever denies me before men, I will disown him before my Father in heaven. Do not suppose that I have come to bring peace to the earth. I did not come to bring peace, but a sword. For I have come to turn a man against his father, a daughter against her mother … a man's enemies will be members of his own household. Anyone who loves his father or mother more than me is not worthy of me; anyone who loves his son or daughter more than me is not worthy of me; and anyone who does not take his cross and follow me is not worthy of me. Whoever finds his life will lose it, and whoever loses his life for my sake will find it" (Matt. 10:32–39).

"If anyone would come after me, he must deny himself and take up his cross and follow me" (Matt. 16:24).

"In the same way, any of you who does not give up everything he has cannot be my disciple" (Luke 14:33).

"Be perfect, therefore, as your heavenly Father is perfect" (Matt. 5:48).

Hard words for wannabe disciples. Such outrageous expectations. Is Jesus serious? Does Jesus really expect a disciple to be "perfect"; one who has set himself or herself aside to live for others; one who lives outside of herself or himself; one who has forsaken everything—friends, family, possessions, everything—and is willing to sacrifice even life itself for others? Can he be serious?

Is that what it means to be a disciple? Does Jesus want us to become outcasts? religious fanatics? wild wandering preachers with nothing but the clothes on our back? If that's what he means, how many disciples are there in our world? None?

The Jesus of the gospels always seems to throw outrageous expectations into the midst of human attempts to achieve homemade standards of goodness. Just when we think we are "pleasing God," Jesus ups the ante.

Remember the rich young man (Luke 18:18ff)? He was a good person. By his own assessment he had kept the commandments since he was a child. Jesus loved him. And yet—Jesus did not welcome him, or take him at his word. Jesus didn't simply ask him to come along with the others and do his best to follow. Jesus dropped a bomb into the middle of his pride and his possessions. "Sell it all and give the money to the poor," Jesus said. "And then come and follow."

All? Surely you must be joking. All of it? Everything I've accumulated over the years? All my stuff? All the things I own and treasure—my collections and possessions? Why they are practically a part of me. They are absolutely necessary to my life. They …

For a true disciple, nothing less will do. But who then can be a disciple? "Who then can be saved?" the frustrated disciples asked. "Jesus replied, 'What is impossible with men is possible with God,'" (Luke 18:26–27).

Finally, all of our attempts to live up to our crafted standards of discipleship fail. When we adjust Jesus' standard of what it means to be a disciple down to our level and pretend that we are "making it," Jesus watches and in effect says to us: "Well done, my child. You have done many good things. You have given much for me, donated time and money (10 percent?), given of yourself on occasion, supported the church, served on committees. You have done very well when compared to the standard. Now all you have to do is give up everything and come and follow me."

Impossible, Lord. Impossible. I cannot do it. I cannot give it all.

Applying the Good News

Impossible? To be sure. But with God, all things are possible.

Our only glory is this: our discipleship is not our self-crafted "disciple uniform" that we manufacture out of our own goodness. Discipleship is God at work in us. As Jesus' disciples, the Spirit is making of us what God would have us be—God creating, the light of the Spirit in us, the hand of God touching others through us.

"For it is not ourselves that we preach; we preach Jesus Christ as Lord. … The God who said, 'Out of darkness the light shall shine!' is the same God who made his light shine in our hearts, to bring us the knowledge of God's glory shining in the face of Christ. Yet we who have this spiritual treasure are like common clay pots in order to show that the supreme power belongs to God not to us" (2 Cor. 4:5–7 TEV).

For we "shine like stars in the universe" (Phil. 2:15).

Who us? Does the apostle mean us—with our

broken-down excuses and faltering attempts at discipleship? Us?

Most definitely! Amid the darkness that threatens to engulf the world, among the lost that we encounter every day, in the middle of the confusion of a million clamoring claims on the hearts of humankind, right there where people live grasping, grabbing, desperate lives—God has set perfect light; God's treasure in common clay pots; God's stars pointing the way.

That's us. Jesus' disciples. That, uniform or no, is who we are.

Very likely, few of us will appear on the cover of a major magazine as examples of great Christian living. Most of us won't win any "disciple of the year" awards. We may never be shunned as fanatics or imitated as paragons. But our discipleship is perfect (being perfected), because it is God's. As the Spirit lives in us, we are effective, active, alive, and worthy disciples.

Are we common? Yes. Unremarkable? To be sure. We are harried, hurried, doing our best. Yet we are the disciples who shine in this dark world with God's light like stars lighting up the skies with eternal hope "to show that the supreme power belongs to God, not to us."

Questions/Activities for Reflection/Discussion

1. Reflect on (share) a time when you were very aware of being marked as a disciple by others. What was that experience like? What was difficult? What was pleasant? What difference did the experience make to you? What was the outcome of the experience?

2. Suppose a group took over the government that was hostile to Christianity. Suppose you were arrested and accused of being a Christian. Would there be enough evidence to convict you? Why or why not? What might serve as evidence? What would others say about you?

3. Think of (share about—but not necessarily with names) the person whom you would call the "best disciple you know." What characteristics most impress you? How does his or her discipleship show? In what way is that person an inspiration to you? What can you learn from him or her?

4. As Jesus was arrested, all of his disciples ran away. Peter even denied him. Yet all of them were brought back as even more effective disciples after Jesus' resurrection. What can we learn from the disciples experience? What truth about Jesus' love can we reaffirm? What comfort can we gain? What intention for our future discipleship can we learn?

5. **Family/Intergenerational:** Make a poster that will identify your home (homes) as a place where Jesus' disciples live. What would the poster say? Add important names, symbols, Bible texts to the poster. Put the poster in a place where it can remind you who and whose you are. Talk often about what it means to be a disciple of Jesus.

Option: Do research on one of the great saints or martyrs of faith. Look in an encyclopedia of church history or read about more recent martyrs (e.g., Stephen, Huss, Bonhoeffer). Write out the story of several of the martyrs and share them with others. What can we learn from the stories of the martyrs?

A drama in two scenes

Characters

Mark/Mary—*elderly male or female, dressed casually*

Doctor—*dressed for hospital duty*

Doris/Dave—*Mark's daughter or son, middle-aged, dressed casually*

Waiting for Me

Scene 1

Scene suggests a hospital waiting room. The room is sparsely decorated with only a few chairs. Mark sits alone, kind of hunched over.

After a time the doctor comes in and sits beside Mark. They exchange greetings, though Mark only looks up briefly.

Doctor: I'm sorry, Mark. Your wife is in a coma. There's not much more we can do.

Mark: And what are her chances? Realistically, Doc, what are her chances?

Doctor: Of course, there could be a miracle, but because of the stroke, the coma keeps getting deeper, her breathing shallower. *(Pause.)* I would recommend that we begin life support in the next few hours.

(Mark looks up at him briefly and then back to the floor.)

Mark: Life support?

Doctor: Respirator, feeding tube, heart monitors.

Mark: You mean you want to help her breathe?

Doctor: And monitor her heart in case of a problem.

Mark: Problem?

Doctor: Sometimes the heart beats erratically. We have ways … to …

Mark: You mean if her heart stops, you want to start it again.

Doctor: It's the only way.

Mark: Only way?

Doctor: It is very likely that her heart will begin to fail as she slips deeper into the coma.

Mark: And what will happen if we do all of that? Will she get better?

(The doctor shifts uncomfortably.)

Doctor: I don't know. To be very honest with you, Mark, I really don't know. But she probably won't improve significantly. She might wake. But there's very little brain function.

(Mark stands and walks away from the doctor. Finally, the doctor stands too.)

Doctor: Mark?

Mark: I don't know, Doc. I don't know what to do. Let me think.

(The doctor leaves, promising to stop back later. Mark is alone again for a time. Then Doris enters rather quickly, throwing a coat on one of the chairs and quickly embracing and kissing him.)

Doris: Dad. How is she? I came as soon as I could, as soon as we got your message.

Mark *(holding her for a moment by the shoulders)*: It doesn't look good, honey. Not this time. We've been through all this before. But this time …

Doris *(backs from him)*: But she's not dying? My God, is she dying?

(Mark is silent, shakes his head.)

Doris *(almost frantic)*: But, Dad. I've got to see her. Can I see her now?

(Doris starts off toward the door and Mark catches her by the arm.)

Mark: She's in a coma, honey. She can't talk to you.

Doris: But I didn't get to see her, before … I didn't get a chance to say to her how sorry I am about …

(The two of them stand looking at each other for a while. Doris turns away, and Mark goes over and sits on one of the chairs.)

Mark: The doctor wants to put a respirator on her.

Doris: Will it help?

Mark: He doesn't know.

(Doris comes over to him, kind of half kneeling in front of him.)

Doris: Dad, we've got to do it. We've got to. She deserves every chance we can give her … every chance …

Mark: And what will happen if we let them put the respirator on and feed her through a tube and keep her heart going? What will we do—prolong all of this?

Doris: But she might get better. She might wake up, and I could talk to her …

Mark: I don't know. I don't want to let her go. I don't want to let her go.

(Doctor returns, and Mark quickly introduces him to Doris. Doctor says that they can go into the room for a few minutes and then leaves again. Doris sits on a chair crying. She shakes her head when Mark puts his hand on her, inviting her to go with him. He goes off alone.)

Scene 2

Stage area suggests a hospital room. There may be a shadowy, inert figure on a bed in the foreground. The sound of a heart monitor would add a sense of reality.

Mark goes and stands by the bed so that he is facing the audience. He stands quietly for a time, reaching out and touching the figure on the bed.

Mark: Hey, Martha, how's my lady? *(He is silent, then speaks more quietly.)* How's my girl? *(Pause.)*

"Your lady's just fine," you'd always say to me. "Just fine and waiting for you to come home to her."

And I always did, didn't I, my lady? Didn't I?

Oh, I guess over the years I was tempted to step away, to go out on my own and chase some of my foolish dreams. I guess I had a chance now and then to run after rainbows or look for someone else to wait for me. But I never did. Do you know, Martha, my love, I never did. Because I knew you were there waiting for me. And I had to come home to you. What else could I do? You were always there for me.

For me!

Oh, Martha, what should I do now? What can I do for you? What would you want me to do?

How can I let you go? How can I? If I let you go, would you think that I had let you down, this one time? Would you think that I was not there for you? Would I leave you waiting for me and not be there, if I let you go? *(Pause.)*

But how can I not let you go? I remember when your father was like this. I remember you looked at me when we were waiting there in the hospital. "Never let them do this to me," you said. "Never let them pretend I'm alive when I'm already gone."

Martha. Martha. Are you gone already? Are you in the hands of the Savior whom you trusted so much to be there to hold you?

Know this, Martha. I pray to God that somehow you will know that if I let you go it will not be because I have tired of your words or the sound of your voice or the touch of your hand. It will not be because our lives wound around each other are no longer a treasure to me. It will only be because I know that even if you are gone— even if I can't touch you and see you and hold you—even if I sit alone in our house and only hear the sounds of our life together in memory, I know we will never be apart.

This I know more surely than anything else in this world, as surely as the promise we made to each other at the altar and the promise we renewed every day. I know that you are there, with the Savior, there in the future that we share and that you are waiting for me.

It will be lonely now without you, my girl. I will call your name and not hear you call back to me. I will wake in the night and have no hand to hold, no warm breath on my cheek to make the darkness seem less cold. But I cannot hold you or make you come back to me.

With all my love, my girl, my friend, I let you go, knowing that we will be together again—where you are waiting for me.

Homily: Cross Point— Choice Point

Theme: How Can I Choose?
Gospel Focus: I can do everything through him who gives me strength. *Phil. 4:13*

Engaging the Listener

The old prospector had spent most of his life searching for gold in the mountains. Each year he'd gather his supplies and head out once more. Each year, at the end of the season, he'd return with little or no gold. One year, things were different. There in a distant valley, he found what he'd always sought—a vein of gold, more than he'd ever imagined. He loaded his donkey with all of the gold it could carry and set off for town.

It had been a dry year. The first water hole he came to was dry. So was the second. Then the third. Now, facing his third day without water, he abandoned the useless gold and realized that he faced death from thirst very soon. He knew of a homestead over a ridge, not too far from where he was. As his last chance, he headed there.

He found some broken, abandoned buildings— and, amazingly, a water pump. He ran, grasped the handle, and pumped with all his might. Nothing. Then, near the pump, he spotted a rock with a symbol scratched on it. Under the rock, he found a small bottle of water. The bottle had a note attached. It said: "In this bottle is just enough water to prime the pump. If you use it to prime the pump, you will have all the water you need." It was signed, "Desert Pete." Now the choice. Should he sip the water in the bottle and try to make it to town, or should he trust Desert Pete, pour the precious water into the pump, and take a chance (gamble with his life) that he would have water?

What would you have done?

We have a fundamental life choice to make also: Do we take the gifts we have been given and keep them for ourselves, or do we give them up in service to God and others, trusting God's promise that we will "overflow" with blessings?

Exploring Our Need

Life is a series of cross points, crossings, choice points. How we answer each one affects every other choice point in our lives.

Choice points abound. The easy ones we call dilemmas—being between a rock and a hard place. Confirmation class students seem to like to try to stump the teacher with questions like these:

- Is it right to tell my wife that her new dress is nice when it is not. Is that a lie? Or more pressing:

- If you are starving, is it wrong to steal bread? What if your family is starving?

- What if you are a doctor? Is it wrong to tell someone an untruth if it might prolong his or her life?

- Is it wrong to break a promise to help someone else?

- Is it wrong if you do something slightly illegal and use the money for something good?

The hardest choices we call crises (from *crucis*—cross)—cross points. They are common and difficult. They bring us to a place where the choices are clear—but the two alternatives seem equally bad. These bring us up short. They bring us quickly to the end of our ability to choose. Both ways seem too dark. Both paths seem blocked.

They are like the choice in the play: What is right? What is best? What must I do?

Many of the Bible accounts have to do with crisis points—choice points. Remember the three Hebrew children. They faced the fiery furnace or bowing down to and worshiping the emperor. Jesus in the Garden faced the choice of drinking the cup or seeking to escape it. Through the centuries, martyrs have faced the terrible choice between faithfulness and death or denial and life.

Some think the Christian life is easier in this regard. They think that we have a set of rules that cover everything and make it easy to choose in every situation. But that is not true. For a person of faith, the choices are not easier. In fact, they may be just the opposite, for when we choose, we consider not only our own desires—but the will of God and the needs of others.

Applying the Good News

And yet, it is equally true, that at these choice points, only the person of faith can make the choice. The old prospector could not make the decision to pour the water into the pump unless he trusted Desert Pete. Only a fool would do that. What has Desert Pete ever done to deserve to be trusted?

But we have a promising God—the God who promised life in Jesus Christ, who comes to us exactly at the point when we run out of our own ability to choose. God comes to us with power and with promise. *(Read Rom. 8:31–39 aloud.)*

We have the gift of life and new life from the one who has done it all, who has done more than earned our trust, who has claimed us and called us back, who has made us his own, who has marked us holy and made us new, who has given us new eyes and a new heart.

How can you risk making a decision when the darkness closes around you? How can you decide when both ways seem dark? We can choose because, in Christ, we can do all things. We are free to act—even to sin boldly, knowing that we are loved and freed and forgiven. Indeed, we can "do everything through Christ, who gives us strength."

And we know that no matter how we choose,

- We will not be abandoned: Jesus says, "I will be with you …";
- We will not be without resources: "The Spirit prays for us because we do not know how to pray";
- We will not be defeated: "[Nothing] in all creation will be able to separate us from the love of God that is in Christ Jesus our Lord."

God's promise and the presence of the Spirit don't make the choices easy—but they do make them possible. They don't make them all right—but they do make them all forgiven. They don't make them all effective—but they do make them all new.

"If anyone is thirsty, let him come to me and drink. Whoever believes in me, as the Scripture has said, "Streams of living water will flow from within him" (John 7:37–38).

Questions/Activities for Reflection/Discussion

1. Reflect on (share) a choice point in your life—a time when you struggled between two ways. What was the struggle like? How did it affect you? How were you able to make the choice? What did God's promise have to do with your choice? How did God's help come to you?

2. Someone says, "I don't believe we really have a choice in anything. God has everything planned. All we do is walk through the steps that have already been laid out for us. Choice is an illusion. God controls everything." How would you respond? What does this kind of fatalism say about personal responsibility? What is the difference between God "knowing" the outcome and "planning" the outcome?

3. When you face a difficult choice, what are the things that you consider. List some of these and share them, if possible. What factors are most important for you? How

do other people affect your choices? How about your faith? What does the promise of God's forgiveness mean as you make choices?

4. David chose to battle Goliath, Moses chose to face Pharaoh, Stephen chose to speak his witness to those who threatened to stone him, and Jesus chose to go to the cross. What other choices from Scripture can you recall or find? What does each say about the person doing the choosing? about faith? about God's promise? What encouragement can you receive from these happenings?

5. **Family/Intergenerational:** Write a letter (adults can help children, or children can use pictures to which adults add words) that you (or your family) should receive the next time you face a difficult choice. Include in the letter words of encouragement, Bible passages, and other helps that are important to you. Share your letters now and save them. Read them again when you are faced with a difficult choice.

The Voice

A dialog in one scene

Characters

Disciple—*Middle-aged male, modern-day clothing*

Voice—*not seen, just a voice from off stage*

Scene

The stage area is empty and dark, if possible. A dim street light suggests a street corner.

Disciple walks along. Long, eerie shadows across stage area will lend reality. Disciple walks tentatively; looks around often; seems worried. All of the speeches of the disciple are spoken in a kind of exaggerated, fretting, almost whining tone. All words from Voice come from offstage, possibly through sound system.

Disciple: I hate these streets at night. It's so dark, so lonely. Not that I'm really afraid, but I do wish they would light them better. I wish they would mark them better or patrol them better. You'd think with all the taxes we pay, they could afford a few lights. What are decent citizens supposed to do to protect themselves in this kind of neighborhood? If I had my choice, I'd never go into this part of town. It's no place for a decent, respectable person to be walking …

Voice: Help me!

Disciple: Did you hear that? That voice? *(He looks around nervously.)* It came from down that alley. *(Pause.)* That dark alley …

(Disciple stands staring, wide-eyed for several beats.)

Voice: Help me, please!

Disciple: Oh, I don't want to hear that. Why does that person have to be suffering near me right now? God, what do you expect me to do? I'm just a plain disciple. Can you really expect me to go back there into that alley? *(Disciple looks again.)* It's so dark and dangerous. I thought you were supposed to protect followers like me. How could you let this happen? *(He frets.)* Oh, how could this happen?

Voice: Help me!

(He starts to walk on.)

Disciple: If I go on, no one will ever know. There's no one else around. Who would know? Who would care? Even that voice in the alley wouldn't know. He doesn't even know I'm here. He'd never know any difference.

After all, I'm not the one who got him into this. He's probably drunk or crazy. Maybe he just doesn't care about himself. Maybe he wants to be where he is. Maybe he likes the dark. Maybe he'd be offended if I came down there into the alley and interrupted his suffering. Some people enjoy pain, you know. Maybe he's one of those. One of those weird people. That's what he must be. A strange person just calling out to see if anyone will respond. He may even be dangerous, for all I know. No one in his right mind would actually go down there, back there, into the dark … would he?

Voice: Please help me! Please!

Disciple: I'm sure someone else will come along. Surely there'll be someone else coming along here—one of those people who work with the poor, maybe. Those people are always looking around for people in need. They might be offended if I interfered in their chance to help this person. And they'd do a lot better job with this than I would. What we have is basically a question of the quality of care. They have training. They know what they are doing. I don't even belong here. I don't have any experience. Surely God wouldn't expect me to actually go down that alley …

Voice: Help me, please! Are you there? Can you help me?

(Disciple begins to search up the street one way and then down the other.)

Disciple: If I could just find someone to go with me … if there were someone else, I wouldn't be so … concerned. And I'm not really the worrying type. I mean, I know how to trust God and all of that. But even good Christians like me know that we're not supposed to tempt God. What would God think of me if I went stumbling down some dark alley and then expected him to save me? I mean that's not even responsible.

Voice: I'm hurt. Can't you help?

Disciple: If I go into the alley, I'll probably get my new clothes all dirty. And what will my wife say then? *(He mimics her in a mocking tone.)* "Two-hundred-dollar suit and you get it all covered with …" *(Pause.)* What if that person is bleeding? What will I do? What can I do? I'm just not good with blood. Anyone who knows me, knows that. I'm the first to faint when someone cuts his finger. God, how could you have this person suffer all over me? I'm not ready to deal with this!

Voice: Please help. Please, God …

Disciple: God? God? God, is this any way to choose someone to handle this? God, if you mean to help this person, why are you sending me? Am I the best you can do? Isn't there anyone else? Anyone else? Me? Am I? Am I the one?

Voice *(very slowly):* My God … my God … why have you left me here alone?

Disciple: Strange. He almost sounds like Jesus, like Jesus from the cross. *(He laughs.)* But this isn't a cross, is it? It's just an alley. And Jesus isn't in dark allies and in the cries of hurting drunks and dope fiends in this rotten city, is he? Jesus is in church, isn't he? Isn't he? Isn't Jesus in church?

(Disciple starts to walk on. He moves slowly down the street, looking back often, listening.)

Disciple: Quiet now. No more calling. Stopped now. I wonder if someone came to help. Maybe it's all taken care of, and I don't have to go. Maybe God found someone else. *(Pause.)* Oh, God, could you please find someone else? Please send someone else. Please …

(He stops, turns, listens. No sound.)

Disciple: God, I ask you, is this fair? Is this right? Can you ask me to go where I don't want to go, to do things I don't want to do? Can you call me to steps I don't want to take, places I don't want to be? Is this fair? Is this what it means to be a disciple?

(He moves again toward the alley, listening.)

Disciple: No one would blame me if I just left—just went on my way. Everyone would agree that you are asking too much … too much …

(With hesitant steps, he makes his way toward the voice, standing there for a time in silence, head bowed …)

Homily: Cross Bearing— Burden for Another

Theme: Bear One Another's Burdens. Gospel Focus: Whatever you did for one of the least of these brothers of mine, you did for me. *Matt. 25:40*

Engaging the Listener

I came from a large, preacher's family. We could not afford "vacations," what with six children and all. Sometimes my dad would volunteer to be a counselor at a youth camp with the provision that he could bring the family along—these travels served as family vacations. Ordinarily, at these camps, we stayed in whatever was called the leader's or counselor's cabin. One time—I was perhaps six years old—I remember, we had arrived late. Just in time for the bond fire—and ghost stories—and my Dad's devotion. The ghost stories scared the wits out of me, what with the shadows and the fire and the darkness. My dad's devotion puzzled me. He talked about the Holy Spirit as the "Comforter." Later we went to the gaunt old cabin, full of small rooms, cracks in the floor, creaking walls, and almost no light. My mother put a couple of us to bed in a back room. I was terrified of the darkness and the silence. I was convinced that small crawling things were coming through the cracks in the floor.

"I'm cold," I called. What else?

My parents rummaged around the cabin. "I found an old comforter," my dad said.

I waited for him to bring the Holy Spirit. Instead, he brought this wonderful, full, feather quilt. As I snuggled under that quilt, with only my nose out—I understood something about the Holy Spirit.

The word translated in the text as comforter becomes "advocate" in most translations. The word does not exactly mean either. It really means "one who comes alongside—to stay."

That came to mean two "come alongsiders":

- In court—one who comes alongside to speak for another—an advocate.
- In illness—one comes alongside to comfort and to care and to support—a comforter.

Exploring Our Need

The focus of this service is bearing the cross of another. We are surrounded by others borne down by crosses. In most cases, they are impressive crosses indeed. They belong to people whose lives are coming apart with troubles, problems, lost jobs, or critical illness. We know that we are called to take up the cross of another. Luther says we are to be "little Christs." But like the character in the drama, we often don't feel qualified.

The call confronts us in the need of another. "Can I do that?" we say. "Can I be all that God wants me to be? Can I be Christ's presence for another? And what if being a little Christ gets me a little crucified?"

Often the call comes, and our response is something like Isaiah's famous response to the call to be prophet: "Here am I, Lord. Send me." But we change it a little: "Here am I, Lord. Please send someone else."

"Lord, it is absolutely true that I am unqualified. I am wandering on the streets of my own darkness, my own crosses. I know all of what you expect. I know all the callings. But I can't seem to get the lines clear. I can't seem to unmuddle the muddle. I can't seem to find the time and the opportunity.

Oh, I know I should do more. But I'm doing the best I can. Is it not enough? Isn't bearing the crosses that I am doing, doing enough?"

The answer is that it is never enough—and always enough.

It is never enough if we see ourselves as "cross removers"—sort of super disciples, sent out into the world to make things right, to remove the problems of people, to make their lives whole again, to solve their problems, to bring them salvation of whatever kind they think they need. That kind of a homemade crusade quickly turns into an impossible burden.

We can never do enough if we see ourselves as burdened "cross lifters," trudging through life trying to heave up these huge crosses that we can hardly get hold of or understand.

Certainly, we fail. If we think that we are going to do it ourselves it will never be enough.

Applying the Good News

But the good news is that whatever we do it will always be enough—because Jesus has already given all. And as we contemplate that gift during this Lenten journey, it becomes clearer: Although God calls us to wondrous deeds and marvelous acts of service—we serve best when we become little Christs and allow the Spirit of God to work through us.

We serve best when we come alongside—and we comfort.

It is what the people around us need. There are plenty of gurus and leaders and preachers and tellers and sellers and all of that telling people what to do and what to buy and how to solve their problems. What most people need is a comforter.

- Someone who will stay with them.
- Someone who will understand.
- Someone who will accept and forgive.
- Someone who will bring hope.
- Someone who will speak the words they don't have words for.
- Someone who will be there.

But the Spirit lives in us and moves us to come alongside of others.

Where will they go, the frightened ones, the troubled ones, the ones in need? Where will they go to find comfort and peace? Where will they find it in a world that bristles with self-ishness and taking and using? Where will they find the comfort—the comforter they need?

"Don't you know that you [actual words are "your body"] [are] the temple of the Holy Spirit, who lives in you and who was given to you by God? You do not belong to yourselves but to God; he bought you for a price. So use your bodies for God's glory (1 Cor. 6:19 TEV).

And when we have comforted any of God's children, when we have done it even for the "least of these brothers of mine," Jesus said, "you did it for me" (Matt. 25:40).

Questions/Activities for Reflection/Discussion

1. Reflect on (share) a time when you were called on to be a "comforter" for someone. How did you feel about the task? What help did you seek or receive? How did you feel when you had finished the task? What did God's promise have to do with your comforting?

2. Think of someone who has been a comforter to you. What was the comforting like? How did it help you? How was God present in the comforting? What was the outcome?

3. A fellow Christian says to you: "I don't believe that God can work through me. I'm just not a good enough follower of Jesus. How could God possibly use me?" How would you respond? What encouragement could you give?

4. Read Ex. 3:7–12; Judg. 6:11–16; Jer. 1:4–7. In each case, someone was chosen for a task. What task? What was the response in each case? What promise was given to the chosen one? What encouragement can we receive from these examples? What promise does God give us as ones chosen to be "comforters."

5. **Family/Intergenerational:** Make a family "comforter." Make it out of paper or

cloth (felt works well). Make it large
enough to hang in your home. On the comforter, put words of promise and encouragement from Scripture, symbols of God's
love (cross, Baptism symbol), and words of
prayers that are important for your family.
Use the comforter to encourage one another and to talk about what it means to be
used by God to comfort others.

The Monster

A monolog

Character

*Middle-aged male,
well dressed*

I don't know about you, but I don't remember much from my childhood. It's all kind of a distant blur. But I do remember the day I grew up—the day I became a man, you might say. Believe it or not, I was only five years old when it happened. That day I met up with the tough, second-grade bully who lived on the next block. He pushed me down and took my nickel—my life's fortune at that time. I ran home crying.

"Daddy," I said. "He pushed me down and took my money."

Daddy, of course, was the one who always made things right. My Daddy loved me. And Daddy was a veritable miracle worker. Daddy could make broken toys work again and produced bags and bags of groceries from the trunk of the car. Surely one so powerful could right the wrong that had been done to me.

But Daddy did nothing. Daddy listened. He wiped my tears and patted me on the head, but he did not do one thing about the bully and about my battered dignity and about my nickel.

My daddy shrank down to reality that day—and I grew. Could it be, I thought, that my dad is afraid of the bully? Could it be that this master of my world, the one who could make money appear in his pockets and command a visit from Santa Claus has been defeated by a seven-year-old low-life from the next block? How could my world hold together if that were true?

A friend—also in kindergarten and also the victim of the same hard-nosed second grader—and I set an ambush for the neighborhood terror. We caught him by a hedge and shoved him into the freshly trimmed bushes before he knew what hit him. And while he was suffering the pains of a hiker in a briar patch, we relieved him of my nickel and his power over us. He never bothered us again. I'm sure he learned something. I know I did. I guess it was the lesson my dad wanted me to learn. If I was going to make it in this world, I was going to have to do it myself. No one was going to take care of me. No one was going to do it for me. No one was going to right my wrongs and fight my bullies. I had to do it for myself.

And I did. Believe me, I was no great student. I got through college by cunning, determination, and a file of exam copies I "borrowed" from the professor's files. If they're stupid enough to leave them where I can get my hands on them, it's their problem—I thought.

And I succeeded in business the same way. Anyone with an exposed weakness became my target. Just as easy as it was to shove someone into the bushes and take his nickel, so it was easy to step up on the backsides of losers.

In truth, I became what you might call a self-made man. I was, I believed, master of all I surveyed and captain of my own fate. I knew how to identify issues, how to find solutions, how to make things work for me. I knew how to force people and problems to conform to my will. There was, I thought, nothing that I could not do, given the chance. (Pause.)

That was, until the monster came to visit me and sat on my bed and smiled at me.

We met at the hospital—the monster and I. My doctor urged me to enter the hospital for the removal of a small lump on my thyroid gland. Nothing to worry about, the doctor said. Ninety percent of these are benign.

I awoke from what was to have been minor surgery with a bandage on my neck that would have done justice to a giraffe. I remember thinking that the pain was so much more than I had expected. The doctor came in and fumbled around at the end of my bed for a while and then muttered something about "quite a malignancy." At that moment, the monster came and sat down next to me.

The monster's name was cancer, and it came to stay with me.

For the first time in my life, something confronted me that I could not overcome. I had no way to trap this thing and push it into the bushes, no way to step it into submission, no way to force it to go away. There the monster sat, waiting, smiling—holding my life in it's scaly hands. It turned my future in its fingers and picked at every thread of joy or hope, every dream, everything I cherished, and there was nothing I could do or say, nothing I could invent or imagine to take it back again.

The monster conquered me. And the terror and the overwhelming grief that I felt was not only because the monster's other name was death—but it was because of the sense of helplessness that I felt when I looked into the eyes of this fearsome beast. This monster was out of the reach of my will, my power, my strength, my wealth, my success, my ability to win. The monster sat there smiling at me—just out of reach—and I was helpless.

In the blackness of my dreams I shouted at it: "Get away from me! Get away from me! Go sit with someone else. Breathe your deadly breath on some other person more deserving of your visit. How can you be here? Who let you in here? Who sent you? Did God send you? Did God send you to bring me down, to hurt me?"

And even in my dreams the monster sat silently and smiled at me.

"God, what have you done? What have I done to deserve this? Have I not been faithful in my giving, attentive to my family, a model of proper living in my community? Have I not tried to be the kind of person I'm supposed to be? At least most of the time? At least some of the time? And even if I have failed, do I deserve this? What about all those others, those cheaters and liars, thieves, fools, takers—those sinners out there? What about them? Why have you sent this thing to visit me?"

And in the silence, still the monster sat and smiled at me.

The pit of my pain and self-pity grew deeper and darker. I could no longer climb the sides of the pit and see the future. The weight of the monster and the shackles of my own fear and anger froze my feet. Buried in that pit, I wept for myself and for my dreams and for what might have been.

And still the monster sat silently and smiled at me.

But there in the deepest place in the pit, there, somehow from the echoes of my memory, these words from Romans came to me: "For I am convinced that neither death nor life, neither angels nor demons, neither the present nor the future, nor any powers, neither height nor depth, nor anything else in all creation, will be able to separate us from the love of God that is in Christ Jesus our Lord."

"Do you mean that, Lord? Do you mean that for me? Not even monsters, Lord? Not even great, grinning monsters who sit beyond my reach and manipulate my future in their terrible hands? Not even my deadly smiling monster?" *(Pause.)*

I live outside the pit now. But not far outside. I'm always on the edge, wondering and waiting. But there's a difference now. Not that the monster is gone. It still waits there firmly fixed in my past and in my present and in my future. It's always there, just out on the edge of my awareness, smiling at me. But now God has placed the cross of Jesus Christ even more firmly between me and the monster.

Most remarkably, I got a gift from the monster, a gift the disease never meant to give me—a treasure I never suspected would be offered by those dangerous, deadly hands. I have finally learned that all of it—the present, the past, the future—all of it—my accomplishments and failures, my abilities and weaknesses, my confrontations with bullies and the visits of monsters—all of it is in God's hands. Even me. Even people like me who live by the illusion that we captain our own fate and determine our own future—even those of us who suffer the visit of the monster—are in God's hands, sealed there by the cross—forever.

And in that promise, from the edge of the pit of my own despair, I stare back at the monster and smile.

Homily: The Cross of Suffering

Theme: God, Why Me?
Gospel Focus: My power is made perfect in weakness. 2 Cor. 12:9

Engaging the Listener

I am going to stand here for three full minutes in silence. Having heard the story of *The Monster,* I want to give you time to reflect on the monsters you have faced in the past. Just take your time. Let the images come to you—even if they are painful. Here in this place of worship, assurance, and support—once again bring into your awareness the face of your monster—that happening that made you say: "Why me?"

[Silence]

Exploring Our Need

(*If there is time, several—you might choose these ahead of time—might briefly tell about the monster in their own lives.*)

Without hesitation we can say: Everyone faces monsters. But what makes a happening, an illness, an event a monster? What makes it more than something that is bothersome or troublesome or difficult.

Events or happenings become monsters because

- they immediately become overwhelming and dominate our lives;
- they bring us quickly to the end of our own power to cope;
- they make us feel alone, abandoned, forsaken—in the pits; and
- they seem out of control—wild, mean, unwieldy; they terrify us.

Applying the Good News

Monsters are bad. No question about it. Experiences with monsters hurt. They are to be avoided at all cost. They break us and threaten to destroy us. They are terrible.

And yet, when we go past the monster, even from a human point of view, the encounter with the monster has value. Even though we may not be able to see it when we are cowering in fear and self-pity before whatever it is that is threatening us, we do learn from the experience.

1. We learn about ourselves. Nothing gives us a clearer, more honest picture of ourselves than an encounter with a monster.

2. We learn the value of the person who will stay with us during the time of crisis. Nothing is so chilling as facing the monster alone. The one who holds our hand becomes valuable for the rest of our lives.

3. We learn to get our priorities straight. Nothing is as valueless in the face of the monster as our accomplishments, our status, our bank account, or our successes. There, as we face that for which we have no answer, we learn the value of time, of health, of love, of people, of the "best things in life."

But even more important, it is the monsters of life that proclaim to us loudly and clearly the good news that God loves us, keeps us, will not give up on us, sustains us, stays with us, and will not let us go.

As we deal with the monster, we learn the following:

1. That the Spirit of God meets us most effectively, most surely, and most importantly at those places where we are the weakest. Indeed, God's strength is made perfect in our weakness.

2. The value of eternal things. When everything of earth fails us (including ourselves) we are left clinging to the eternal promises of God.

3. How effectively God works through other people. The word of comfort and encour-

agement does not come to us in blind inspiration from the sky. It comes through the people around us who love us, comfort us, stay with us, and will not give up on us.

4. That only God can be depended on. Everything else fades.

5. That even monsters give way to the power of God in Jesus Christ. "Nothing in all creation," says St. Paul (and that includes monsters) "will ever be able to separate us from the love of God which is ours through Christ Jesus our Lord." The victory is already ours.

And so, in a strange reversal, the very points of our lives at which we are the most vulnerable, the most broken, the most helpless become those places where we learn most about ourselves, about the value of others, and about the meaning of God's promises. It is at the point of our weakness that we see, hear, know, and experience what is most important in life. It is at the point of our failure that we learn the permanence of God's love for us in Christ. It is at the end of our strength that we learn the eternal effectiveness of God's strength for us. It is at the point of our death that we learn the eternity of God's life for us.

Monsters abound. Some will overtake us. Some will confront us. Some will bring us to the end of our ability to cope. And all will cause us to cherish ever more surely the love of God in Christ Jesus our Lord.

Questions/Activities for Reflection/Discussion

1. Reflect on (share) a monster you have faced. What was that monster like? How did you feel as you dealt with it? What made it a monster for you? How did others help you face the monster? How did your faith help? What was the outcome of that facing?

2. The Bible is full of passages of promise and hope. What is your favorite? Find, reflect on, and share, if willing, an important Scripture for you. If nothing comes to mind right away, look in a concordance or Bible dictionary. Or look at favorites like Psalm 23, Psalm 121, John 10, and 1 Corinthians 15. Think or talk about what the promises of these texts mean to you now and in times when you face the monsters of life.

3. Read as much of the story of David and Goliath (1 Samuel 17) as you have time for. Think about or talk about what you can learn from the account. What does it say about monsters? What does it say about faith? about God's promises? about the outcome we can expect? about action in the face of monsters? If you were teaching the story to children, what would you want them to learn about God?

4. "The greatest monster is death." Agree? Disagree? Why? What makes death terrible for us? What is our reaction to death? How can we face death? What do God's promises have to do with our ability to face this monster?

5. **Family/Intergenerational:** In times past, people used to decorate their house with religious words, pictures, and symbols in the belief that they would help keep away the forces of evil. We no longer trust in objects to protect us, but some of these items can remind us of God's love, protection, and care. Make a "monster fighter" decoration for your house. You might do a design on paper, make a cross out of wood, or make a banner out of felt. Work with several others to create something that you can hang proudly in your home. Share your creations and talk about how they remind you of God's promise.

Peter's Last Visitor

A dialog in one scene

Characters

Peter—*late in his life, tattered, dirty clothing—as if having spent some time in a dungeon*

Cecelia—*middle-aged Roman noblewoman; her bright, white attire and jewelry contrasts sharply with Peter's dress*

Scene

The stage suggests a dungeonlike cell—bare except for a stool and a wooden box (or another stool).

Cecelia enters with the clank of a metal door. Peter looks up, gets up, and moves quickly to her.

Peter: Cecelia! (*He is surprised to see her; he embraces her quickly, then backs away and bows slightly.*) My lady! How did you come here? Are you alone? Why did you come? How did you get in here?

Cecelia: So many questions, Peter? I came to see my friend. I got in with the keys that rich Roman women have always used to open any door. (*She jingles a coin purse she has tied to her waist.*)

Peter: Oh, I'm so glad to see you. I was hoping …

Cecelia: Hoping someone would come, but probably not me. Is that what you were going to say, Peter? Probably, in that list of people you'd like to have come and spend your last evening with you, I was not there near the top.

Peter: No. That's not true. If I had a list of people I'd like to talk to once more before tomorrow—before whatever happens tomorrow—you would be right up there at the top.

(*During these exchanges, Peter returns to the stool and offers her a place on the box or stool opposite him. They lean toward each other as they speak.*)

Cecelia: Peter! You are such a liar. Why would you want to see me? I'm not one of your followers. I'm not in the little group of—what do you call them—Christians—who follow you around and think you're so wonderful.

Peter: I admit I'd like to see some of them again, just once more—Timothy and Justin and Ruth and Lydia—all of them. But I know they're with me, even if they can't risk coming. I don't know about you, my lady. Where are you?

Cecelia: Don't be clever, Peter. I'm right here with you.

Peter: Are you? Are you with me? And when they call for the count of the believers, will you stand with me?

Cecelia (*turns away and is silent for a while*): I … I don't know, Peter. I don't know what I will do. I'd love to believe like you do—to trust in your God the way you do. But I can't. I can't make myself …

Peter: But that's just it, Cecelia, you don't have to make yourself. You just have to *let* yourself, and the Spirit will help you believe.

Cecelia: Believe in what? In that wandering nobody of a teacher that you follow? In some mysterious God who does not even have a face? Should I follow a God whom I cannot even see, one who leaves his people to die in the arenas and to be crucified in public? Is that the one I should believe in?

Peter: Yes. Exactly. For all your protests, my lady, he is the one who is calling you, the one who brought you here tonight. The one who seeks you.

Cecelia (*stands and moves away from him*): Do you realize that all of this is a little crazy. I came to visit a condemned man who is waiting to be put to death by the emperor—one who will be crucified in the public square in the morning—crucified upside down, some say. And you are trying to help me? Does this make any sense? (*She turns to face him, speaking down to him.*)

My friend, you are either the most remarkable man I have ever met, or you are simply crazy. I don't know which. In any case, I came bringing you an offer. I do not come by accident. The emperor himself sent me.

Peter: Sent you? A woman?

Cecelia: Oh, he trusts me. (*She laughs.*) He thinks I'm not smart enough to double-cross him. He thinks that, even if I tell others about what we planned, no one would believe me. He thinks I'm safe. Stupid but safe.

Peter: And what do you think, my lady?

Cecelia: It doesn't matter what I think. I care about you. God knows why—but I care. And the emperor cares too—in his way.

Peter: About me? About this pretentious Jew, this ignorant fisherman who's been a thorn in his side all these years? He cares about me?

Cecelia: You know, Peter, as odd as it may seem, I think he does. At least he's jealous of you—of your strength and your wisdom. I know he'd like to get out of this without having to put you to death.

Peter: For my sake or for his?

Cecelia: Both, maybe. In any case, he's aware that if he puts you to death, he'll make a martyr out of you. People will idolize you.

Peter: Instead of him. Is that it?

Cecelia: Perhaps. For whatever reason, he's prepared to offer you your life. All he wants is that you promise to stop preaching about this Jesus and publicly recognize what he calls "the emperor's divine authority."

Peter *(laughs):* That's all he wants?

Cecelia: Just that. And he will let you live. He'll simply banish you to some other country and leave your followers alone.

Peter: That's quite a deal. But you can tell him that I cannot do it. *(He grows quieter.)* Even if I were so weak as to fail to stand up to what awaits me, I would never stop speaking of my Savior.

Cecelia: You? Fail? I can't imagine that, Peter. I think it is your strength, your absolute conviction, the peace that surrounds you that fascinates the emperor—I know it fascinates me.

Peter: Enough to believe, my lady? Enough to trust?

(She is uncomfortable now, pacing almost.)

Cecelia: I could trust in you, Peter. But your God?

Peter *(stands and moves after her):* You don't know what you are saying. Trust in me? I'm no one. I'm nothing. I'm not even worthy of the privilege of dying on the cross like he did. I've failed so often. *(Pause.)* So often …

Cecelia: You? I can't see you failing. You stand so sure, speak so confidently, even before the emperor. You, Peter?

(Now he turns away. He is remembering something painful.)

Peter: My lady, you do not know this, but when Jesus—our Lord—when he was taken captive before he was crucified, he was abandoned by all of his followers.

Cecelia: Even you, Peter? Surely not you. You must have gone with him.

Peter: Oh, I went with him, all right. Right to the place where he was on trial—right to the very court of the high priest. I thought myself so brave that I had even swung a wild sword at one of the guards who came for him. I thought myself so wonderful that I had volunteered—volunteered, mind you—to take whatever was coming to Jesus.

And yet … *(very slowly)* and yet, when they looked at me, there in the courtyard, when they pointed fingers at me, accused me, I failed. I could not even mention his name. I refused to admit I even knew him. Not only did I not fight for him, not defend him, not stand with him—I denied him. I did exactly the thing he warned me I would do. I failed him completely. I saved myself—saved myself for my time of weeping.

Cecelia: I just can't believe that, Peter. I can't believe that you would fail. And if you did, how is it that you still follow him? You must have come to yourself and come back to him, sought him out, and made things right again.

Peter *(laughs):* I wish that were true. If I'd only been strong enough to come to him again. But even after he rose from the dead, I could not bring myself to approach him. I longed to be with him again—but I could not even look him in the eye. And yet … and yet, he came looking for me. He came after me, sought me out, and comforted me. I was the one who had failed, and he found me. He found me to give me a place to belong, a task to do. He loved me enough to seek me. *(Pause.)*

You marvel at my conviction. It is not because I know I am strong enough to stand up to the emperor or to the soldiers or to the pain or to the dying. Left on my own, I would most certainly fail again; I would go to pieces and say anything to save myself. But what gives me strength is this—I am more certain of this than anything in the world—if I fail, even if I fail, even if I turn my back on my Savior and deny him, even if I collapse into a bundle of fear and trembling and deny all who believe in me, even then, he will not give up on me. He will still come and find me and make me whole again.

Cecelia: How can you be so sure, Peter? How do you know?

Peter: Because he has always been there for me and the others who love him. He has found me so many times and put me on my feet every time I have fallen. Because he has chosen me—a poor illiterate fisherman, good only for cleaning nets and complaining—and made me one of his leaders. Do you know how miraculous that is? How wonderful? How unbelievable?

Cecelia: Not one of the leaders. You are *the* leader. There is no other. And the emperor is smart enough to know that if he kills the head of this cult, the rest will eventually just fade away. They will lose heart, and the movement will disintegrate.

Peter *(laughs):* Well, that might be smart politics—but it won't work. You can tell him from me that he cannot kill the head. He can kill me. I mean nothing. He can put me to death in whatever way he wants—and it won't matter. The head is Jesus Christ, and he's already been put to death and already risen to new life. The emperor can do nothing.

Cecelia: But they need you. Those poor followers, those poor persecuted people who follow you so blindly. They need you, Peter. How will they be able to go on without you? *(Pause—more quietly.)* How will I be able to go on without you?

(Peter comes to her and takes her gently by the shoulders, speaking directly to her.)

Peter: My lady, you don't need me. I am nothing but a voice. Don't depend on me. Depend on the one who lives in me, who wants to live in you, who lives so that you can live now and forever. Depend on him.

Cecelia *(turns away, scornfully):* And then I can join you on the cross or in the arena with the lions? Is that what you offer me, Peter? Terrible death.

Peter: I don't know about your death. Certainly all of us will die. But I do know this, that without him, you will be condemned to a terrible life. I offer you a life that is full enough so that death, when it comes, will be a completion and not just a robber.

Cecelia: If only I could believe, Peter. If only I could believe.

Peter: I know this, my lady: The God who loves you and brought you here, the God who gives you life, the God who gave himself on a cross for you, who believes in you, who cherishes you—that God will not let you go until you are safe in his arms, in his heart, in his care forever.

Cecelia: Oh, Peter. You are such a fool. Such a beautiful, wonderful fool. You stand hours from your own death and speak to me of life. Here in this dungeon with nothing to look forward to but torture and hatred and pain, you comfort me and tell me of dreams of life that can never be.

Peter: Never, my lady? Never be?

Cecelia: Never for me. Not for me, Peter.

(She begins to leave, then turns and comes back over to him. She embraces him and holds his hands.)

Peter: I will pray for you, my friend. I will pray that the God who is chasing you will be there when you fall and raise you into what he wants you to be.

Cecelia *(almost angry):* Pray for me? You fool. I'm not the one for whom the soldiers will be coming in the morning. I'm going back to my safe house. Perhaps you should pray for yourself.

Peter: Oh, no. I have the easy part. I only have to face death—a death that has no power over me—you, my friend, have to face life.

Cecelia *(after a pause):* And what shall I tell the emperor?

Peter: Tell him that if I could help him, I would. But that I do forgive him—and tell him that God loves him.

Cecelia: Even him?

Peter: Yes, even him.

(Once more she comes over to him; she kisses him quickly on the cheek and then turns to run out.)

Cecelia: Peter, my friend. Pray for me. Pray for me.

(Cecelia goes out quickly. Peter hears the door clank shut and then returns to his stool, bends over his hands, and resumes his prayers.)

Homily: The Final Cross

Theme: Will I (Will God) See My Life As Ended or Completed?
Gospel Focus: For to me, to live is Christ and to die is gain. *Phil. 1:21*

Engaging the Listener

I found my friend Maggie in the midnight-darkened hallway of the hospital. She sat bending over her pain. I knew she would be there. For days she had stayed there and waited for the five minutes each hour she was allowed to go in and be with her Harold.

They had never been apart, she told me. In the 55 years they had been married, they had never spent a night apart. Through all the years on the farm, through the birth and raising of their children, through the illnesses they had both suffered, they had never been apart. Now he was dying. I think she knew it, but the doctor wanted me to tell her that her beloved Harold could not last the night.

"Why don't you go on home," I suggested. "I'll sit here for a while."

"I can't go," she said.

I held her hand, and we prayed.

The nurse came by. "You can go in now," she said. "Don't forget the gowns and the masks. We don't want the infection to spread."

Harold didn't seem to recognize the two, green-shrouded figures that came to his bed—at least not until Maggie took his hand, moved her mask, and touched her lips to his cheek.

I said a prayer out loud, but all the time she was whispering to him. She kept her head right alongside his on the pillow—talking to him like she belonged there.

Later, in the hallway, she was weeping.

"What did you say to Harold?" I asked—more to cover the silence than to get information.

"I told him I loved him and that I would stay with him."

"You know he's very ill. He may not be with us in the morning."

There was a long silence. "I know," she said. "He knows he is dying too. He's afraid a little. I can tell by the way he holds my hand. But it's all right. I know he's all right now. I told him that it will be Easter in the morning."

I did not know what to say. It was November. Had she forgotten? "Um. It's not really Easter," I offered.

"I know, Pastor," she said patiently. "But for us it is. We've practiced celebrating Easter together for all of our years. Now for Harold and me, tomorrow is *our* Easter."

Exploring Our Need

If I took a vote for a subject for discussion, I suppose that death would not rank up there very high. Death doesn't seem like a particularly inviting subject, even for a worship service. We live in a strange society—we are used to daily hearing and seeing death, and yet we deny it.

In some ways we have become callous to death. We treat it as entertainment. By the time they are 16, our children have seen some 20,000 murders on television.

Yet, in our daily living we rarely speak of death. And when we do, we often try to make a joke of it:

- "I've used up my sick days, I'm calling in dead."

- In a cemetery, a certain Oriental man was placing a tray of food on the grave of his wife—a custom in his culture. Nearby, another man began to laugh at him. "When do you expect that person to come up and eat that food?" he called. The Oriental man replied: "About the same time the person in that grave comes up to smell your flowers."

Or we use soft words for it—"he passed on," "she went to her reward." Or the one I heard recently: "irreversible cessation of cerebral, psychomotor, and physiological activity."

And death is very near: we wake short of breath; a car swerves and just misses us; a quick pain shoots through our chest.

Death brushes us. Its cold breath touches us before we are aware of it. It is never far, like a silent companion, pressing on us, just beyond our reach.

One of the moves in modern psychology is to make death "natural." Since it comes to all life, they tell us, we should learn to accept it, embrace it; we should learn to make death our friend.

But we know that is a lie. Death is not a friend. It is an enemy, a robber, a thief. The death of a loved one throws us into a pit of grief so deep that we become convinced that we are in the depth of the pain of separation that may never be healed.

And still, we don't want to deal with our own death.

Applying the Good News

Look at Jesus' death. In a way it is remarkable—in a way it is not remarkable.

Thousands had been crucified. Millions had been martyred, suffered injustice, or were cut off in their prime. Sad? Yes. Terrible? To be sure. But not that out of the ordinary.

And there have been others who went into death with dignity. History is full of stories of those who went to their deaths in a way that inspired awe in others.

Neither was Jesus the first one to go out with "famous last words." History reports many.

What is remarkable is what he said in those last words. He said very plainly: "It is complete." Note that he did not say, "It is over," as if out of relief. Nor did he say, "I made it," as if out of pride. He said, "It is complete."

Over the years, I have sat with many on their deathbeds—young and old. Some meet death well; others fight against it. But the difference is not age. Those who meet death well are those who have a sense of completeness about their lives. In the face of the great robber, they seem to say: "It is complete."

My life is complete. Certainly everything may not be done. Perhaps there are many things I feel I yet would like to do, but my life has a wholeness about it. That wholeness is related to purpose, related to God, and related to the meaning of my life.

That's what Peter meant in the drama when he said,

> "I don't know about your death. Certainly all of us will die. But I do know this, that without him, you will be condemned to a terrible life. I offer you a life that is full enough so that death, when it comes, will be a completion and not just a robber."

That's the hope that Maggie had as she waited in the hospital for Harold's death. She lived an Easter faith: an unshakable conviction that every day—not just that last one—is an Easter event. By God's grace in Jesus Christ, we are able to live with the outrageous conviction that every death, every ending, every tomb, every pit of despair—produces a new beginning.

That's what sets us apart as Christians dealing with the crises of life. We are not simply on a quest to escape, as many are. In Christ, we overcome.

Does the death of a loved one hurt us? Do we fear our own death? Can grief and separation drive us into the pits of grief? Can the crises of life drive us to the ends of our ability to cope?

Certainly. Most certainly, we are powerless in ourselves in the face of the great robber—death itself. But we are not defeated. For we are convinced that even death is overcome. Even that great robber must yield to new life. And that conviction gives us a sense of purpose that allows us to say in the face of the great thief: My life is complete, in Jesus Christ.

And as foolish as it may sound to the people of the world, we say with St. Paul, "For to me, to live is Christ and to die is gain."

"Where, O Death, is your sting? The sting of death is sin, and the power of sin is the law. But thanks be to God! He gives us the victory through our Lord Jesus Christ. Therefore, my dear brothers, stand firm. Let nothing move you. Always give yourselves fully to the work of the Lord, because you know that your labor in the Lord is not in vain" (1 Cor. 15:54–58).

Questions/Activities for Reflection/Discussion

1. "We are people of the Easter faith." What does that statement mean to you? What does Easter have to do with everyday living for you? In what way do you give evidence of your Easter faith? How can you share it more effectively?

2. Reflect on (or actually draw) your picture of death. What does your picture say about your understanding of death? What makes death fearsome? What has God given you that enables you to face death? Put the picture of the resurrected Jesus over death. What difference does it make?

3. Reflect on (share about) a death that was particularly difficult for you. What feelings did you have to deal with? What attitude did you have toward God at that time? Who helped you? How did God's promise come to you? What was the outcome of your experience?

4. 1 Corinthians 15 is called the "resurrection chapter." Read it (aloud if possible). As you read, pick out the words and phrases that are most important for you. Discuss those. What words of hope do you find? What words do you want to remember? Make a point to memorize some of those passages.

5. **Family/Intergenerational:** Imagine that you could leap several generations into the future. You are watching a group of people reflect on you and your congregation and family. What would you want them to remember? In what way would they say your lives were "complete"? If they made a poster or banner remembering how God worked through you, what people and events would be on the poster? What words of thanksgiving? Talk about it: What hope for the future do you find in reflecting on how God can "complete" your life?

Good Friday
A Drama

My Son—a drama for Good Friday, explores some of the elements of repentance, forgiveness, acceptance, love, and sacrifice in terms of the relationship of a son to his father. There are aspects of a human parent/child relationship in the drama and aspects of God's relationship to us. The drama can be used to engage people in preparation to a proclamation about God's unconditional love for us in Jesus Christ. Some may wish to discuss the drama and what it says about our relationships to each other and to God.

My Son

A drama in one act, one scene

Characters

Son—*about 21, dressed casually*

Father—*about 50, in business suit*

Officer—*a uniformed guard*

Scene

The stage suggests a visiting room at a jail or prison. The only light in the stage area shines down on an institutional-looking table and two chairs. The tone of the scene is gloomy. If possible, a side light casts the shadow of prison bars across the stage.

Son sits at the table. He seems to be waiting. He sits with his head bent down, staring at his folded hands. Father enters from side behind Son. He stands behind his son for a moment before speaking. He seems to struggle for words.

Father: Son, I'm sorry I couldn't get here sooner. I wanted to be … I know you wanted me here.

(Son looks up at him briefly and then back to his folded hands on the table.)

Father: I really didn't hear about the accident until yesterday—and then I was in the meeting. I couldn't leave. You know how it is. They depend on me. I couldn't get away until …

Son: The everlasting meeting.

Father *(fretting):* I know I should have been here, but I couldn't get away. The meeting …

Son: Dad, that meeting has been going on all my life. It keeps you whenever someone needs you. My mother needed you—and you were always at the meeting.

Father *(defensively):* That's not fair. I've never let you down. I've always been there when you needed me. Haven't I always come through for you?

Son: Yeah, like the time I got hurt in the game. You were right there, weren't you?

Father *(still defensive):* I was in Europe. What do you expect? I got you the best doctors. Didn't I make sure you had the best care?

Son *(sarcastically):* Yeah, the people in the white coats were marvelous.

Father: What could I do? I couldn't fly back in the middle of the conference, could I? I was running the thing. And all you had was a concussion. You were out of the hospital in a day.

Son: No, Dad—it was a night. I was in the hospital one long night with the faceless people and the sounds that echo in the halls …

Father: Listen, what do you have to complain about? You got the best of care. I paid the bills, like I always do. It was *your* idea to play on the football team. What do you expect me to do about that?

Son *(angry):* I know. It's my fault. My fault that I got hurt. My fault that I was in the wrong place at the wrong time. I know I'm the one who always messes up.

Father: And I've never held that against you. Haven't I always been there to get you out of your little scrapes? Even when you did it yourself.

Son: That's it, Dad. You've always paid the bills and the fines and bought off the ones I hurt. I remember how you took care of the neighbor's broken windows and the woman who got her car a little dented.

Father: And even more. When you got arrested—both those times—wasn't I there when you needed to get out?

Son *(sarcastically):* Yeah, Dad, right on the spot. You paid the fines and paid for the damage and paid the lawyers and paid the piper. It's true. I've got the "payingest" most-distant father in the world.

Father: How can you say that? After all I've done for you? Don't I always get you the best? You're the best-dressed kid in school. You've got the best car. You're getting the best education.

Son: The best things. Things, Dad, to pay me off so I wouldn't bother you and to buy off your conscience so that wouldn't bother you either.

Father: What do you mean, buy you off? I'm the one who stayed. I didn't run off like your mother did. I didn't turn my back. I made a good life for you, gave you a decent home, gave you the best of everything. How can you turn on me? I'm the one who …

Son: Put up with me all these years?

Father: This is crazy. You're the one who's in jail. But this feels like I'm on trial. What do you want me to do—go and stand in front of the judge for you? Do you want me to say that I'm the one who drove the car, that I'm the one who drank too much, that I'm the one who left the scene of the accident? Do you want me to stand there and pretend that I'm the guilty one? Aren't you the one who did the driving and the drinking and the …

Son: Killing?

Father: I wasn't going to say that. The policeman told me that the woman was driving too slowly and she was on the wrong side of the road when she turned. It wasn't all your fault. You can plead innocent. You did your best to avoid the accident. You aren't guilty …

Son: Would that make you happier? Would that ease your conscience? *(Pause.)* The truth is, I am guilty. I drank too much, I drove too fast, I ran the light. I killed the woman …

Father *(placating):* But you don't have to tell the judge that. What good is it going to do for you to go to jail over this? It's a shame that a life was lost. Is it going to make it any better if you lose yours too?

Son: You know, I think I've come to the conclusion that there is not much to lose. *(Remembering.)* I woke in the hospital yesterday morning with the accident still in front of me. I kept seeing the face of the woman in the car just at the second when the headlights went out. I saw her look at me—her eyes filled with terror and question and accusation. And then I looked up. They had put a mirror over my head. I could not help but stare into my own eyes. And I saw … not guilt or innocence or question or confusion … not pain or fear … I saw nothing. Nothing there. Nothing behind the eyes at all. I've lived 21 years, and do you believe it, there's nothing there.

You claim to care. What is there to care about? What is there to reach out to? I looked into my eyes and saw nothing at all.

Father: You're being too hard on yourself. You're not nothing. Lots of people care about you. You have friends …

Son: Who love my red car and my full wallet.

Father: You've got … others … people who care.

Son: Like?

Father: Well, me for one. I care. Don't I show you that I care?

Son: Yeah. You call me on the phone once in a while, when it doesn't interfere with your meetings. You put a note on the refrigerator when you want me to do something. You call to me sometimes when you come home in the evening. Oh, yes, Dad. Do you ever care!

Father: But I do care. I've given and given.

Son: Money and excuses and ways out of trouble. Yes, you've given all those. You've given when people would think you were something less than a caring parent if you didn't give. But when have we shared something, Dad? When have we done something together just because we enjoyed each other? When have we been just dad and son. When have we laughed together and walked in the woods or spent the day at a game or just shared the joy of each other's company?

Father: But I've been out there earning a living for you. I did it for you. I made the money and paid the bills for you. Where would you be if it hadn't have been for me? You'd probably be in some reform school or in some prison somewhere. I kept you out of trouble. I made it possible for you to get on with your life even when you were guilty. Can't you see that's caring? How could I continue to forgive you and get you off the hook if I didn't care?

Son: Oh, give me a break! You may have given a million dollars and half your life, but you never forgave me. You never forgave me for getting between you and my mother, for cluttering up your life with obligations, for being there and making demands. You never forgave me for making you feel guilty because you were not a real father to me. You never forgave me—you resented me, you hated me. Somehow I think that empty nothingness in me is exactly what I've gotten from you all these years.

Father *(angry):* So now it's my fault. You hurt, so it's my fault. You suffer, so I'm responsible. You don't like yourself, so I'm the bad guy. Well, I'm not going to accept that. I did my part. I gave you everything you needed. I cared, even if you don't think so. I'm not the bad guy in this plot. I did what I could. I've …

Son: Dad, you seem so blind. You gave because you were supposed to. You helped me because you were expected to. You never loved me. You never gave yourself to me. You never let me in.

Father: That's rubbish. That's meaningless talk. If I never let you in, then why didn't I shut you out when I could have? Why didn't I give up on you when you kept getting in trouble? If I never let you in, why did I hang in there and keep on forgiving you and keep on taking you back?

Son: You still don't understand. You never forgave me. You never forgave me for being me. That grudging overlooking of my faults and failings is not forgiving. That's not forgiving because it doesn't hurt. It doesn't come from the heart, from inside where the pain is so intense that it cannot be turned off. You cared enough about your image as a "loving" father to excuse me. You've never loved me enough to forgive me.

(Father comes to son and attempts to put his arm around him.)

Father: My son, I always cared. Even when I didn't show it, I cared.

(Son pulls away.)

Son *(very angry):* Just go away and leave me alone. I don't want you. I don't need you. I've made my own way for years. Why should you care now? Now it may not even matter. Just go away. Take care of your meetings and yourself and your precious house. I don't need you! I don't want you!

(Father, hurt, begins to move away. He moves toward the edge of the light, head down. He stops there, seemingly unable to move. He stands, facing away from son in silence for a long time. Finally the son looks at him.)

Son: Are you still here? I told you to go. You don't want to be here. Just go. Just leave me alone.

Father: I can't go. I can't take the steps away from you. I can't.

Son: But you're no good here. This time you won't be able to buy me out. This time you can't stand in the background and pay my way for me. I have to face this alone.

Father: I still can't go.

Son: Why? What do you want here? You don't even want to be here? You don't have anything for me, and it's sure I have nothing for you. Why do you stay?

Father: What do you expect? What do you expect of me?

Son: I expect nothing. I need everything. Dad, don't you see that I need you to love me? I need you to look at me, at the emptiness and pain that is in me, at all of the failings and faults that contribute to who I am—and love me still. Love me just because I am your son. Love me just because I live in your heart and cannot be shaken or moved or taken from there. I need you to love me.

Father: But I do …

Son: Can you say it, Dad? Can you say you love me?

Father: Say it? Don't I show it day after day? Don't I show how much I care?

Son: Can you say it, Dad? Can you put it in words.

Father: Son. My son. I … I … I love you.

Son: Do you, Dad? Do you? Or are those just words?

(A police officer enters as they stand and stare at each other.)

Officer: I'm here for Bart Michaels.

(Father and Son both respond.)

Officer: I mean the Bart Michaels who was in the fatal accident—the one who's supposed to go before the judge.

Father: I'm the one.

Officer: Really, I thought it was the younger one.

Father: No. It's me. I'm the one who's responsible. I'm the one who will stand before the judge. I'll take the punishment.

(Father begins to go off with the officer. Son puts his hand on his arm.)

Son: But, Dad. Why?

Father: Because I love you and will always love you. Because you are my son and no one will ever take you out of my heart. Because you are mine, and I will not let you go. My son—there is nothing you can do, no pain you can cause me, no disappointment you can put me through, no word you can say—you cannot run far enough or turn your back often enough to make me stop loving you.

Son: Dad, I'm sorry. Forgive me.

Father: Forgive you? My son, you are already forgiven.

Homily: But You Do Matter

Text: What a wretched man I am! Who will rescue me from this body of death? *Rom. 7:24*

Engaging the Listener

This is a true story. It came through the Religious News Services. I have simply changed some of the names.

The members of a Methodist congregation in New England wanted to help a prison parolee to resettle and thought it might be a good idea to invite a rehabilitated ex-convict to speak to the church. The pastor suggested a name: Mark C.—a name that startled the congregation. Mark was the man who had shot and killed the pastor's son in 1987.

So in a few weeks, in the church basement, the pastor and Mark taught the members of that congregation a lesson in repentance, forgiveness, and the promise of new life in Christ.

Mark had been on parole for two years, after serving time for the killing. The pastor's endorsement had helped convince the parole board to release him. Explaining his actions, the pastor said, "My son's life had been taken, but I didn't want my own life destroyed by bitterness and anger."

The pastor was in the courtroom when Mark was sentenced, and "when I heard him say … that he was sorry for what he had done, I was moved" the minister said. On the first anniversary of his son's death, the pastor wrote a letter to Mark in prison. He expressed anger over the death of his son, but also appreciation for Mark's seeming remorse. "As hard as these words are to write, I forgive you," the pastor wrote.

Mark said that he had been angry when he saw the return address on the letter and, at first, had refused to open it. However, it haunted him, and he took it to a prison counselor who read it and urged Mark to read it. "Tears started running out of my eyes. I didn't know how to handle that," Mark said. "When I did the killing, I thought my life was over. But that night I knelt down next to my bed and asked God for forgiveness."

Humble in the face of Mark's gratitude, the pastor told his congregation, "I could not offer forgiveness without the strength that God gives me. I also knew that I could not go on living with anger and bitterness. I had to do something."

How many of us could have done the same? Forgiveness that comes from the place of pain, that goes against our instincts, that is offered in spite of the anger and bitterness that tempt us when we are hurt—is terribly difficult. By human standards, it is perhaps impossible.

Exploring Our Need

Perhaps we make a mistake in our worship services. In our eagerness to communicate the free gift of God's forgiveness in Christ, we make it appear very easy. At the beginning of almost every worship service we say some form of confession. And the pastor responds with words of assurance that our sins are forgiven.

(Take time to look at the form of confession and forgiveness used in the liturgy for the service you are doing.)

But it seems so easy. "Lord, I sinned."

"That's all right," the pastor seems to say. "There's nothing to it. God forgives you."

And we give the impression that forgiving is like excusing. "Forgive me," we say to the person we bump. "It's all right. It doesn't matter," comes the response.

Is that forgiving? Is that what God is doing? "Forgive me, God." And God responds: "It's all right. It doesn't matter."

Doesn't matter?

If that is true, Jesus' going to the cross doesn't matter. If God excuses sin, what point is there in the death of Jesus?

"My God! My God! Why … ?" Jesus cries in agony from the cross. And if God overlooks sin, if God pays almost no attention, if it doesn't matter—then why indeed?

Applying the Good News

In the play, the father thought that he was forgiving his son every time he came to bail him out. He thought that giving things to his son or being there to try to make things right for his son was enough like forgiveness to make a difference.

But it was not. The son felt unloved because the father by his actions said, "It doesn't matter." And in saying so, he also said, "You do not matter."

The father came to realize how terribly hurt the son was by his hidden message of nonacceptance. The things he bought could not convey the love he had for his son. The only gift that would finally let the son know he was loved and lovable was the gift of himself. The father was willing to take the punishment for the son, not because he excused him—but because he loved him so much that he could not turn away.

That is the picture of God's love for us. God loves us so much that, in Christ, he cannot turn away—even though we deserve to be turned away from.

The message of Good Friday is not that our sins, our sinfulness, our failures, our mistakes do not matter. We are not announcing a great excusing program here for those who are troubled by sins of the past. We are not here to tell you that God is saying to you that you do not matter.

In fact, you do matter. What you have done matters. What you need, what you are, matters. In truth, you matter so much that God is willing to step into your place. In Jesus Christ, he takes our broken, empty, failed selves to himself and in his self-giving shouts to us over the din of the world and our own self pity: "You do matter. In fact, you matter so much that I will give myself for you."

The result of that final giving is not more guilt, but freedom. Finally, we can look ourselves in the eye and say, "I do matter. Not because of what I have done or because of what I have accomplished, or because of what I have earned, but as a free gift, God gives himself—and I matter that much. Thank God!"

Thank God for his incredible gift. Amen.

Questions/Activities for Reflection/Discussion

1. Reflect on (share) a time when you gave the gift of forgiveness to another. Describe the experience. What did the giving do for you? What did it communicate? How did the forgiving create healing?

2. Realizing that forgiveness is not excusing, but is a deep and sometimes painful giving of self, read Peter's question in Matt. 18:21–22 again. Why is what Jesus commands ("seventy times seven") so difficult to do? Where can we get the strength to forgive and forgive again?

3. "I just can't forgive that person for what he or she did." Suppose you heard those words from a friend or relative. What would you say? How could you help that person? Suppose the words were on your own lips. What kind of help would you want? What healing would you need? How would God's forgiveness be involved in that healing?

4. Look again at the form of confession and absolution used in your congregation. Work together to put that confession in your own words. What exactly are we saying when we "confess" to God? Rewrite the words of forgiveness spoken

by the pastor. What words do you need to hear when you confess? Share your restatements with others.

5. **Family/Intergenerational:** Agree that at least once during the coming week you will speak words of confession and forgiveness to each other. Seek opportunities to speak words of confession and the words of forgiveness. Meet at the end of the week and talk about the experience. What healing happened because of the forgiveness? How can you make regular confession and forgiveness more a part of your life together?